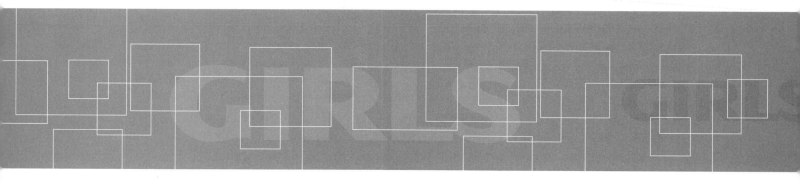

Girls

10 Gutsy, God-Centered Sessions on Issues That Matter to Girls

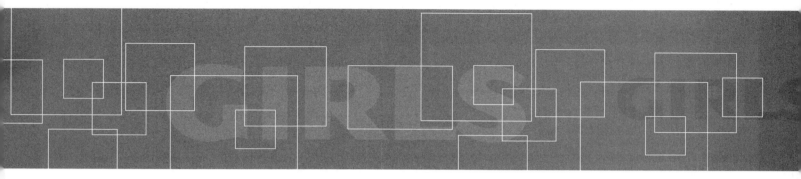

Girls

10 Gutsy, God-Centered Sessions on Issues That Matter to Girls

Helen Musick　　　Dan Jessup
Crystal Kirgiss

ZONDERVAN™

GRAND RAPIDS, MICHIGAN 49530 USA

ZONDERVAN.COM/
AUTHORTRACKER

Youth Specialties

www.youthspecialties.com

Youth Specialties

Girls: 10 Gutsy, God-Centered Sessions on Issues That Matter to Girls

Copyright © 2002 by Helen Musick

Youth Specialties products, 300 S. Pierce St., El Cajon, CA 92020, are published by Zondervan, 5300 Patterson Ave. S.E., Grand Rapids, MI 49530.

Library of Congress Cataloging-in-Publication Data

Musick, Helen, 1957-
    Girls : 10 gutsy, God-centered sessions on issues that matter to girls / Helen Musick,
    Dan Jessup, Crystal Kirgiss.
        p. cm.
    ISBN-10: 0-310-24128-6
    ISBN-13: 978-0-310-24128-7
    1. Church group work with youth. 2. Teenage girls—Religious life. I. Jessup, Dan,
1958- II. Kirgiss, Crystal. III. Title.

BV4455 .M87 2002
248.8'33—dc21

                                                    2001039097

Edited by Vicki Newby and Dave Urbanski
Cover and interior design by Razdezignz

Printed in the United States of America

06 07 08 09 • 18 17 16 15 14 13

Contents

A letter from Helen Musick

A girl learns early in life that there's one thing she doesn't want to live without…other girls. I'm not sure if it's in our DNA or by divine design, but girls need girls.

Jane Ann was my best friend. We did life together. My mom knew where to find me if I wasn't at home—and her mother knew the same. We ventured through the early adolescent years together. We did all those important firsts together. We went to our first grade school party and danced with real boys. We shaved our legs together for the first time.

Jane Ann and I hung out together, but when we wanted company, advice, or someone to listen, we would head to Mrs. Byron's house. Mrs. Byron was the mother of two small children and went to our church. For some reason, she liked us. She was always happy to let us come in and visit while she was making dinner. Sometimes, the events of the day would be covered and questioned. Other days, we'd just sit silently and watch her. We knew Mrs. Byron loved God. She didn't tell us Bible stories or quote Scripture in the kitchen. It was simply by her interest and concern for us that we could tell there was something different about her life. And at just the right moment, when we were ready to listen, she taught us Truth, gently, leaving us with a sense that God mattered in our lives and we mattered to God.

During the past 20 years of my life, I've made it my goal to be Mrs. Byron to young girls. More recently I find myself thinking, "I'm too old for youth ministry." I was fine with girls thinking of me as their friend or big sister, but now I'm older than most of their moms. I find myself wondering at times if God can use me to make a difference. That's when I remember Mrs. Byron.

You can be a Mrs. Byron, too. There's something special about gathering together a group of young gals who are searching for guidance on life issues and spiritual challenges. This curriculum is designed to help you and give you confidence as you open your home, your heart, and your life to girls. It's been our goal and desire to help you make that gathering stronger and more significant by helping you address key issues teen girls face and question.

Our prayer is that you sense the presence of Christ in a way that transforms not just the girls who find their way to you but your own life as well.

Helen Musick

WELCOME

Welcome to Girls

Why a book for girls only?

Because, to whatever extent guys are different from other guys and girls are different from other girls, to an even greater extent, guys-as-a-whole are different from girls-as-a-whole. Our—Helen's, Dan's, and Crystal's—combined years of youth-work experience, marriage, and parenting provides endless evidence for this fact, and it was confirmed during an intense strategy and development retreat in preparation for this curriculum. Let's just say that the men and women of this team—while wholeheartedly agreeing on the purpose, topics, and goals of this book—tended to approach the discussion in, well, slightly different manners: in general, the men were more likely to crack jokes, and in general, the women were more likely to consume diet soft drinks.

Teen girls (in general, usually, as a rule, by and large, for the most part, on the whole)—

- tend to be more verbal than guys
- tend to be more relational (having a small group of close friends) than guys
- tend to be more outwardly emotional than guys
- tend to be attracted to the opposite sex based on what they feel, not what they see
- tend to like chick-flicks more than guys (hmm…)

…to name a few.

By framing and tailoring these lessons specifically to girls and their unique God-given design, we want to encourage your girls to ask questions, discuss, argue, learn, disagree, and offer opinions more freely than they might in a guy-girl setting.

What's in Girls for you?

Each lesson includes the following—

Delvin' In
Data, anecdotes, background and other stuff to get you started.

Warmin' Up
A mixer to grab your girls' attention and get off to a great start.

Many activities can be enhanced with appropriate music. The right tunes can add energy and enthusiasm to active games and elevate them to rockin' good times. Some activities call for soothing music that enhances reflection. Keep a CD player and selection of CDs available, and use them to your advantage.

Diggin' a Little Deeper
Your choice of group, video, or individual activity, each intended to draw your gals into the topic and explore it. Use one. Use any two. Use all three.

Gettin' into the Word
A study of God's Word directly related to the topic.

The Gettin' into the Word Bible study includes a list of Nudgers. What are they? Thoughts, ideas, prompts, and questions to help you and your group think about the Bible more deeply. Here are some ways to use them—

For the leaders—
Read through the Bible passage and Nudgers throughout the week preceding the lesson to get your own creative and insightful thoughts flowing.

For the girls—

- After introducing the Bible passage, read Nudgers to your students while their eyes are closed, encouraging them to visualize and think about the story in a new way.
- Read appropriate Nudgers before each individual discussion question.
- Print copies of Nudgers for all your students to reflect on while the Bible passage is being read.
- During the lesson give each girl one Nudger to reflect on. Let your girls share their thoughts with the group.
- In pairs, have the girls read the Nudgers one at a time and discuss together.
- Make copies of Nudgers for the girls to take home and think about during the week.

Takin' It to Heart

A closing prayer or activity to wrap up the session.

Quote

Quotes taken from the Bible and contemporary sources, the topic-relevant quotes are scattered throughout the lessons. Use them to prompt your own reflection, post them in your room, or draw them into the discussions.

On the Home Front

A handout to send home with your girls—for journaling during the week.

Additional handouts are located at the end of each lesson.

We've added something new!

All the handouts for *Girls* are posted at www.YouthSpecialties.com/store/downloads password: women, where you can access them for free!

- **Plain Text** Just plain ol' text. Format- and graphic-free so you can change the words or add new design. Accessible no matter what computer or word-processing program you own.
- **Rich Text Format** Customizable text (no graphics) with basic formatting such as bold and italics.
- **MS Word 95/6.0** Customizable text (no graphics) with basic formatting such as bold and italics.
- **Adobe PDF** The designed handout as it appears in this book (not customizable). Print one copy to take to the copier or print all the copies you need for your group on your computer's printer.

Preparation: Ya gotta love it!

These sessions are guidelines for you—ideas, suggestions, and possibilities. We know a thing or two about girls as a whole, but we don't know your kids. You know your girls best, what activities will work with them, what concepts need emphasis, how active they need to be, how closely they've already bonded. So use our ideas to make the sessions your own. Tweak, add, delete, substitute, adjust.

Of course, you can manage this best when you plan and prepare in advance. We've tried to help you, to make easy for you. But if you try to read the material in the car on the way to the meeting, you're bound to experience some disappoints. Enhance your ministry to teen girls by reading the sessions in advance and spending a bit of time preparing.

TIP

The final session (week 10) is a time for celebrating, a time for affirming, a time for blessing. Even as you begin to read through the first session, look ahead to Session 10. Give yourself plenty of time to pull together a support team and to plan a memorable event.

Keeping your perspective

A lot of information is available about youth ministry—what it is, how to do it, how to do it better, how to survive it, and how to succeed at it.

We'd like to boil it down for you to a few simple thoughts—

- Ministry is not a thing, a theory, or a theology. It's a way of life.
- Ministry is not something you're trained to do (though training is good.) It's something you're born, or rather reborn, to do.
- Ministry is not something that happens at youth group, at the high school, or during ministry hours. It's something that happens everywhere, all the time.
- Ministry is not about what you do. It's about who you serve.
- Ministry is simply this…loving God and loving others.

Peace from all of us,

Crystal Kirgiss

Your *If-Only* Self
I'd be happier if only...

🔾 THE ISSUE

The world's primary message to adolescent and teen girls is *you might be happy and content, but you'd be happier and more content if you changed your appearance, changed your fashion style, changed your friends, had the right guy, and (especially important) spent a lot of money on a funky pair of shoes.*

---

introduction
Delvin' In

When you think about the challenges that face today's teenaged girls, what comes to mind first? Anorexia? Depression? Pregnancy? Divorced parents? Sexuality issues? Yes, yes, yes, yes, and yes again. The list of challenges is endless and many vie for first mention. When psychologists, parents, and youth workers finally have one problem identified, labeled, and possibly under control, another one rears its ugly head. That pattern is likely to continue in this age of whirlwind change and millisecond advancements.

Though adolescent girls face numerous challenges as they mature, perhaps the greatest one has to do with physical appearances. In the best-selling book, *Reviving Ophelia*, author Mary Pipher says, "At thirteen, many girls spend more time in front of a mirror than they do on their studies. Small flaws become obsessions. Bad hair can ruin a day. A broken fingernail can feel tragic . . . Girls feel an enormous pressure to be beautiful and are aware of the constant evaluations of their appearance . . . 'Every day in the life of a woman is a walking Miss America Contest'" (*Reviving Ophelia,* Mary Pipher, Ballantine, 1994, page 55).

Guys have a hard time understanding this, probably because they aren't continually bombarded with images of a perfect body, perfect hair, perfect complexion, perfect everything. "I hate it when girls talk about their weight," said one high school guy. "Who cares, anyway?" Nice sentiment, but it's a sure bet that he *does* care about a girl's weight, and it's even more sure that the girls in his school know it.

Take some time this week to flip through a few teen magazines. Pay attention to the commercials that are aired during prime time. Glance at all the beauty and dieting products that are sold in every grocery and discount department store. If it's been a while since you've been a teenager, you need to spend a little time recalling those feelings of "I'm not good enough. I'm not pretty enough. I'm not thin enough." If your teen years aren't too far in the past, you can probably recall those feelings with ease.

Before you point your girls toward their true identity (the subject of the third session), help them recognize the false identity the world is selling them. And then clarify that beauty is not an evil thing in itself, rather it is the *worship* of beauty that leads down a dangerous path.

opening activity
Warmin' Up

Who Am I?

You'll need—
- **Index cards or small pieces of paper**
- **Masking tape**
- **Marker**

Write the names of well-known females on the index cards— one name on each card. You can use athletes, musicians, actresses, politicians, authors, local celebrities. The names should all be familiar to your girls. If you have a group of five or less, have one girl come to the front. Then tape one name card on the wall behind her so that the others can see it but she can't. Explain the activity like this—

The card I just hung up has the name of a famous female on it. [Name of girl] has to figure out whose name is on the card. She may only ask yes or no questions. She can direct her questions to the entire group or to any individual in the group. Her goal is to name the person in as few questions as possible.

Have a volunteer keep track of how many questions she asks. Repeat the process with the other girls.

If you have a group of six or more, tape an index card with a name written on it onto the back of each girl. Then give an explanation like this—

Each of you has the name of a famous female taped on your back. It's your job to figure out who she is by asking each other yes-or-no questions. For example, you can ask, "Is my person an athlete?" but you may not ask, "What kind of work does she do?" Once you've asked one question, you

have to move to a different person— one question per person at a time. You can answer one question at a time from each person you ask a question of. The goal is to see who can name her famous female first.

Let the students mingle for several minutes while asking questions. When each person has figured out her name (or after 10 minutes), pull your group together and ask questions like these—

> What kind of questions were most helpful in identifying your person (questions about occupation? appearance? age?)?
> What makes your person famous?
> What do you admire about your person?
> If your person is well-liked, what do you think draws people to her?

— exploring the topic —

Diggin' a Little Deeper

Transition with something like this—

We mainly identify people by appearance and by occupation. Each woman we identified in the game is famous because of what she does and is probably described as something like "gorgeous" or "talented, but not very pretty."

The world's idea of personal identity can be pretty shallow. It's all based on exteriors. Exterior appearance. Exterior activities. Exterior fame. Let's take a look at how the world identifies and defines women.

quote

Closet Space (kläzət spas) *n*, No matter how much a girl has, there is never enough.

Clothes (kloz) *n*, Something else girls never have enough of.

Hair Spray (har' spra) *n*, A substance girls spend 15 minutes applying to their hair to achieve five minutes of hold.

Makeup (mak' up) *n*, What girls spend two hours putting on to achieve the natural look.

from Mrs. Webster's Dictionary, by Lisa Cofield, Debbie Dingerson, Maia Lacher, and Lea Rush, Great Quotations Publishing, 1993

Choose one or more of the following activities.

option [group activity]
Who Wants to Look Like a Million Dollars?

Divide your girls into groups of two or three. Explain to them that you're going to take a look at how the world defines young women. Hand out several magazines, pens, and one copy of **Who Wants to Look Like a Million Dollars?** (page 18) to each group. Give them about 10 minutes to look through the magazines and fill out the worksheet as a group. When the groups have their lists made, come together and discuss the results with some questions—

> **You'll need—**
> • A stack of teen and fashion magazines
> • Copies of **Who Wants to Look Like a Million Dollars?** (page 18) one for each group
> • Pens

➤ What's the main focus of the ads you saw?
➤ Why do you think people respond to these ads?
➤ What motivates you personally to buy some of these products?
➤ In what ways do the advertised products define who you are?
➤ What if-only's do these ads target, and what are the promised results? For example, "If only I had a better complexion, I would be more popular."

Then summarize by saying something like this—

The way advertisers get your attention is by displaying a beautiful model and trying to convince you that all women should look that way. If only you looked that way, your life would be better than it is now. If only your life were better than it is now, you'd be happier and more popular than you are now. We all know that's not how it works. No shampoo, no diet pill, no makeup, no piece of clothing can make you look like the person in that ad. Do you know that models, with their beauty and body shapes, represent only about one-tenth of one percent of the world's population? (And often photographs of them are digitally improved!) It's impossible for most of us to look like that. But many of us keep trying anyway.

option [video clip discussion]
Clueless

Show the clip from *Clueless* when Tai, the new girl at school, is rescued by two clueless but fashion-savvy girls who transform this plain Jane into a supermodel. A lil' warning: there's a somewhat audible utterance of the "s" word during this clip—your discretion is advised. (There are also make-over clips in *She's All That* or *Grease* if you prefer.)

> **You'll need—**
> • *Clueless*
> • TV and VCR

Don't love the world's ways. Don't love the world's goods. Love of the world squeezes out love for the Father. Practically everything that goes on in the world—wanting your own way, wanting everything for yourself, wanting to appear important—has nothing to do with the Father. It just isolates you from him. The world and all its wanting, wanting, wanting is on the way out—but whoever does what God wants is set for eternity.
—from 1 John 2, The Message

0:24:50 "I met a really cute guy."
0:26:54 Tai admires herself in the mirror as the "Supermodel" song ends.

It wasn't so long ago that you were mired in that old stagnant life of sin. You let the world, which doesn't know the first thing about living, tell you how to live.
—from Ephesians 2, The Message

Follow up with some discussion questions—

> Why is there so much pressure on teen girls to look, walk, and act a certain way?
> Do most teen girls change something about their appearance or behavior to fit our culture's expectations for them? Explain. What characteristics are most commonly changed?
> Do girls put more energy into having the right look or into the having the right personality? Why do you think that?
> Why do you think so many girls buy into the idea, "If I can just get the right look, then things will be great"?
> Can you think of a movie or TV show where the heroine doesn't fit our culture's definition of A-okay? Tell about her.

option [solo activity]
If Only

Make sure each girl has a copy of **If Only** (page 19), pens, and a Bible. Give them about 10 minutes to answer the questions. Gather the group together and ask some follow-up questions—

You'll need—

- Copies of **If Only** (page 19), one for each student
- Pens
- Bibles

> Are your if-only's all possible? Why do you think that?
> If your if-only's really happen, how would your life change?
> Think of the activity you love to do the most and that brings you the greatest happiness. Can your if-only's make you happier than that?
> Is it possible to ignore advertising messages? If yes, how can it be done?
> What's the hardest part about rejecting the view of beauty and success promoted through advertising?
> What does the Bible say about our culture's ideas on beauty and success?

Gettin' into the Word

The Hemorrhaging Woman
Mark 5:24-34

Move into the Bible study by saying something like—

You'll need—
• Bibles

One word describes our culture's way of identifying each of you as individuals—change. Change your hair from straight to curly, curly to straight. Change your hair from brown to blonde or blonde to red. Change your weight from whatever you weigh now to something lighter. Change your eye makeup from bold to natural, natural to subtle. Change your clothes from casual to chic, chic to urban. Change this and that and everything else and then maybe, just maybe, you'll be beautiful, successful, and happy.

The trouble is, each of us is unique. No matter how much I change, I can't become another person. Neither can you.

There's a story in the Bible about a woman who, according to the world, was neither beautiful nor successful. In fact, people avoided her like the plague. Let's look at it.

 Nudgers (nuj´erz) *n.* a tool used to gently push teens toward new insight

> Imagine being known as unclean to everyone around you.
> Imagine having no physical contact with anyone for 12 years.
> Imagine having spent all your time and money looking for a cure, with no success.
> Imagine the risks for an unclean woman to enter a crowd of thousands.

> Imagine the fear when Jesus said, "Who touched me?"
> Imagine the moment when all eyes turned to you, the woman known as unclean.
> Imagine having the chance to tell Jesus your story, face to face.
> Imagine having Jesus look in your eyes and call you "Daughter."

Read Mark 5:24-34 to your students, or ask one or two students to read it to the group. Use the following to help process the story—

> ➤ Describe what the woman's life might have been like for the past 12 years.

> ➤ Even though the woman's condition was internal, how might it have affected her externally?

> ➤ What might the woman have been thinking and feeling when she first entered the crowd? Explain your thoughts.

> ➤ In what ways does Jesus show this woman that she has worth and value in his eyes? (You may want to point out that during the time of these events, women were treated as property, had virtually no legal rights, were considered uneducable and unreliable as witnesses in court, and would not be spoken to by Jewish men in public.)

> ➤ How may the woman's view of herself have changed after talking with Jesus? Why do you think so?

> ➤ What do you think affected the woman more—being physically healed or meeting Jesus? Explain.

Finish with something like this—

The world tries to define us by its own standards. Because those standards are nearly impossible to achieve, many of us are left feeling unattractive, unaccepted, and substandard. But the world is wrong. Your worth is not measured by how you look, what you wear, or who your boyfriend is. Don't let the world tell you who you are. Let Jesus tell you. You are valuable as you are because God created you and loves you.

— closing —
Takin' It to Heart

Before you pass out **On the Home Front** (page 20), explain how you would like your girls to use it—perhaps as homework or as an optional devotional guide during the week. If you express expectations, be sure to include follow-up during the next lesson. Distribute the handout as your girls are leaving.

You'll need—
• Copies of **On the Home Front** (page 20), one for each student

⊙ TIP
Look ahead to Session 10, Through the Looking Glass. To have a special closing celebration, allow plenty of time for planning, delegating, organizing, and preparing.

All handouts are posted at
www.YouthSpecialties.com/store/girls
in plain text, Rich Text Format,
MS Word 95/6.0, and PDF formats.
Buyers of *Girls* can use them for *free!*

* Who wants to look like a million dollars? ☺

>>>> Page through teen and fashion magazines to look for ways advertisers try to sell you their products. List the product being advertised in the first column, list the product's promise if you buy or use it in the second column, and finally list the implied result.

The Product what you should buy	The Promise what it will do for you	The Possibilities how your life will be better
Face cleanser	Perfect complexion	You'll have guys knocking down your door to go out with you.

>>> Take the information from your lists and create the MILLION DOLLAR WOMAN. Describe her, including appearance, career, abilities, lifestyle, social life, hobbies, and anything else you want.

❶ If Only ································

Think about you. What would you like to change about yourself? How do you think the change would affect your life? Write your ideas in the chart below. For example, "If only I had a perfect complexion, then more people would like me."

If only...	Then...

Now read Ephesians 2:1-3 to see what God has to say about the world's if-only's. Do you have any *cravings* that have to do with your physical identity? Maybe you always crave new clothes. Maybe you crave the affections of a certain guy. List those here.

Read 1 John 2:15-17. What worldly desires do you think most teenage women have? What do women your age boast about?

♦ On the Home Front

Read the story of the hemorrhaging woman in Mark 5:24-34. Think or journal about these questions—

What parts of you feel unclean, unaccepted, or less than perfect?

If you had the chance to tell Jesus your story face to face, what would you tell him?

PRAYER
Put Your Hands Together

Dear God,
It's hard living in today's world. There are so many pressures to look and be a certain way. It usually leaves me feeling dissatisfied. Sometimes it even makes me hate myself. Help me remember that the world's message is wrong. And dangerous. Then help me look for happiness and contentment in the right place—with you. Amen.

THOUGHT
For Your Gray Matter

The world wants you to fit into the crowd;
Jesus helps you stand out from the crowd.

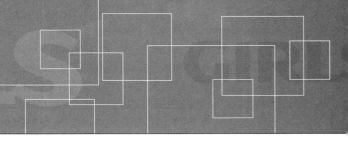

2 Your *I-Am Self*
The me only I can see

⊘ THE ISSUE

Somewhere inside every teenage girl—if you dig deep and search wide—there is a unique individual who may be significantly different from who she *appears* to be. That unique individual deserves to be searched for, identified, and celebrated.

┌ introduction ┐
Delvin' In

To anyone who works with adolescent and teen girls, it's quite obvious the affect our culture's definition of beauty and success and perfection has on them—just think back on some of your discussions from the first session. Chances are that many of the girls in your group believe they would be happier if they could change certain

> **quote**
>
> "You are unique. You are a human being, but you are not just any human being. In all the history of mankind there never has been, nor will there ever be, a person exactly like you. You have feelings and thoughts that no one else has ever felt or thought before. You have a unique dignity: of all the millions of people that God might have created in place of you, he chose to create you."
>
> — *Vincent P. Collins in* Me, Myself and You
> *(Abbey Press, 1974, page 103)*

things about themselves. It's hard for them to believe otherwise when the world's messages are so strong and convincing and repeated so often.

But underneath the outer surface of every young woman—though perhaps, for the more mature and confident ones, it has actually starting creeping out into the open—is an individual who has some strong ideas about who she is, who she wants to be, what she believes, and what she values. Many girls get in touch with this "someone" by journaling, by having late-night chat sessions with a special friend, or by listening to their hearts when the noise of the world quiets down enough.

There's been much ado about the gospel of self-esteem in recent years. Many think positive self-esteem is one of the necessary ingredients for a successful life. Others think that too much self-esteem takes the focus from God's leading to a person's own power. It's likely that both are right to some degree. Certainly we want our young women to rely on God for their strength, their wisdom, and their salvation. But don't we also want them to have the self-esteem that comes from knowing they have as much value as the next person—even if the next person is a male? In *Newsweek* magazine (November 2, 2000), author Sharon Begley points out that not only do a person's stereotypes affect how they treat other people ("I believe girls are weaker than boys"), but it also affects what the objects of the stereotype believe about themselves ("I am a girl, and since girls are weaker than boys, I must be weaker than boys"). In essence, many of the world's stereotypes about females become self-fulfilling prophecies.

Mary Pipher writes,

Just as planes and ships disappear mysteriously into the Bermuda Triangle, so do the selves of girls go down in droves… In early adolescence, studies show that girls' IQ scores drop and their math and science scores plummet. They lose their resiliency and optimism and become less curious and inclined to take risks. They lose their assertive, energetic and "tomboyish" personalities and become more deferential, self-critical and depressed (*Reviving Ophelia,* page 19).

This single session cannot solve the problems mentioned above. The goal of this session is for each of your students to take a step toward figuring out who she is deep down inside—not who the world says she is, not who her parents say she is, not even who her friends say she is. This session will give the girls a chance to look inside at who they are, what they love, what they dream of, what they believe, and then say to that person, "You are me, and I am you, so we'd better start facing life as one person."

> After reading the ideas added to your list, how have your thoughts about yourself been influenced?

◎ TIP

If you notice someone struggling with her list, give her some ideas based on what you know about her. No one should feel that she's too boring, too plain, or too blah to make a list.

─ opening activity ─
Warmin' Up

Uniquely Me

Before the girls arrive, hang the paper on the walls all around the room.

You'll need—
- **Paper, one sheet for each girl**
- **Pens**
- **Masking tape**

Give everyone a marker. Have each one choose a piece of paper and write her name across the top. Give them two to three minutes to brainstorm what they think is unique about themselves. For example—

> Heart-shaped mole on my left arm
> My great-grandparents came from Transylvania
> Can guzzle a Coke in 30 seconds and win any burping contest
> Can double curl my tongue

This should be a fun activity, not a contest. You can help set the tone by having a list of your own that includes serious, fun, crazy, and weird things.

After the girls have made their own lists, have them to go around the room and add one idea to all the other girls' lists. When they've finished, give them a chance to read their own lists with its added items. Then gather together for some discussion.

> What was the hardest thing about writing your lists?

─ exploring the topic ─
Diggin' a Little Deeper

Move into the next activity with a comment like this—

Last week we talked about how the world defines young women. This week we're going to look at how you define yourself, not on the outside, but on the inside. Who are you really? Does anyone ever get to see that person? Is that person comfortable with who she is? Does she hide her true self from other people? Let's find out.

Choose one or more of the following activities.

option [group activity]
I'm All About

Give each girl a copy of **I'm All About** (page 27) and a pen. Give the group a few moments to look over the list. Explain the activity to them like this—

You'll need—
- **Copies of I'm All About** (page 27), one for each girl
- **Pens**
- **12-inch strips of leather cord, one for each girl**
- **Colored beads with holes large enough to be threaded with leather**

Sometimes we're so busy and stressed out that we lose touch with ourselves.

We begin forgetting who we are on the inside and what we believe. Look through the list on your handout and circle the 15 items that are most important to you.

Give the girls several minutes to do this. For some, this might be difficult (for example, the girl who begins her day with, *Blue jeans or khakis? Sweatshirt or blouse? Doc Martens or sandals? Blue eye shadow or green? Hair down or hair up?*) It might help if you tell them that by choosing 15 from the list, they're not saying that the remaining 10 are unimportant to them—just not *as* important.

After a few minutes, ask them—

- ➤ What was the most difficult thing about eliminating 10 things from the list?
- ➤ How did you decide which things were most important to you?
- ➤ In everyday life, how do you choose between two things that are both important to you?

Ask for one or two volunteers to read their lists.

Now the fun really begins. Tell the girls that from the 15 they chose, they must now narrow it down to 10. Ignore the moaning and groaning. It's part of the job. Give them a few minutes, then ask for a volunteer to read her shortened list.

Repeat the process. Narrow the 10 down to eight. Then the eight down to five. Then the five down to three. And finally, have them circle *the* most important thing on the list. (If you're short on time, you can reduce the list from 15 to six to one.)

Make sure your teens are given the freedom to follow their own instincts. You don't want anyone to think that God must be their number one choice just because they're in this group. Obviously your girls are all at different places in their spiritual and emotional growth. This is a great opportunity for you to get a glimpse into their hearts.

After they've made their final choice, say something like this—

We all have things that are really important to us. And what's important to us determines how we act, the words we say, the thoughts we think, the choices we make, and the way we relate to other people. Even though we each have many things that are important to us, there's one thing that's the most important. Identifying that one thing can help you understand yourself.

Now have the girls put stars by their top five choices. Place the beads in the middle of the group so the girls can see the different colors. Say something like this—

Look at your top five choices and at the beads. For each of your choices, pick a color that will remind you of that choice. For example, if you chose

You're blessed when you're content with just who you are—no more, no less. That's the moment you find yourselves proud owners of everything that can't be bought.

—*Jesus, from Matthew 5*, The Message

friends, you might want to pick one of your school colors. If you chose family, you could use the color of your house. If you chose God, you could use white to represent that he is light. Any color for any choice is okay. Just be sure to make a connection for yourself that you can remember.

All quotes in this book that are denoted by age are from *Live and Learn and Pass It On*, by H. Jackson Brown Jr., (Nashville, Tennessee: Rutledge Hill Press, 1991, 1992). Reprinted by permission.

"I've learned that when I grow up, I'm going to be an artist. It's in my blood."

—age 8

Let the girls take some time picking the colors of the beads. They can ask each other for ideas or advice. Not only is this activity about individual soul searching, it's also about communicating. It's important to move from knowing oneself to sharing that self with others.

After they've chosen their beads, let each girl share the connection between her top five choices and the bead colors. Listen carefully. You'll learn what's important to each teen.

Hand out the leather cord and tell the girls to use the beads to make a bracelet. The easiest way to do this is to center the beads on the cord, tie a knot by each outer bead so they won't slide around, and have a neighbor tie it on the wrist. For an adjustable and removable bracelet, tie the cord as shown in the diagram—

Then ask the following questions.

> Why is it important to identify the things you value the most?
> Have you decided on the five things you value the most or has someone else—like your parents, friends, school, church—imposed them on you? Talk about that.

> How might identifying the things you value affect your daily life? Your decisions? Your friends? Your relationships with your family? What you want to do with your life after school?

Wrap up the activity with a few comments—

Each time you look at this bracelet, I want you to be reminded of who you are. Those five beads represent things that are vitally important to you, and because of that, they're a reflection of who you are, what you value, and what you believe in. You are much more than your outer appearance or what you have accomplished. You are heart and soul and mind and spirit.

option [video activity]
Little Women

Show the clip from *Little Women* when Jo reveals her true self to Laurie, a young man she's just met.

You'll need—
• *Little Women*
• TV and VCR

0:15:20 Jo has just backed into the curtained area.
0:17:24 "Are you shocked?"

> Describe Jo—her voice, face, emotions, body language—as she was telling Laurie her dreams.
> Are people like Jo and Laurie afraid of being in the crowd? Embarrassed about who they are? Self-confident? Shy? Something else? Explain your thinking.
> Why do some people, like Jo and Laurie, prefer to watch things from behind the curtain instead of being out in the middle of the action?
> Do young women like Jo have unrealistic hopes for the future? Behave bravely

because they have a vision for the future? Talk about that.

➤ Do most teens have dreams for the future?
➤ Do they have plans to get there? Or do most feel lost or unsure about who they are and who they want to be? How can the lost or unsure change that? Explain your thinking.

➤ Does your dream for the future seem possible? Talk about that.
➤ What might your parents think of your dreams? Why?
➤ What might God think of your dreams? Why?
➤ What can you do now to start preparing for the future, whatever it may hold?

option [solo activity]
10 Years Down the Road

Before focusing attention on the handout, say something like this—

You'll need—
- Copies of **10 Years Down the Road** (page 28), one for each girl
- Pens
- Bibles

No one knows what her future holds, but most people have dreams about what they hope it holds. God does have a plan for your life. But that doesn't mean sitting back like a couch potato and waiting for life to whap you over the head, shouting, "You over there! Time to head off to the airport! Hustle! Hustle!" Instead, you can take a look at the way God made you and the desires he's put in your heart to start moving ahead.

Do you want to stand out? Then step down. Be a servant. If you puff yourself up, you'll get the wind knocked out of you. But if you're content to simply be yourself, your life will count for plenty.
—*Jesus, from Matthew 23,* The Message

Give a copy of **10 Years Down the Road** (page 28), a pen, and a Bible to each student. Give the students several minutes to read through the handout and respond to the questions. When they've finished, gather as a group to talk.

— Bible study —
Gettin' into the Word

The Woman Who Anointed Jesus' Feet
Luke 7:36-50

Nudgers (nuj´erz) *n.* a tool used to gently push teens toward new insight

➤ Imagine the horrors of a prostitute's life.
➤ Imagine what holier-than-thou men thought of a prostitute.
➤ Imagine something that expresses your inner thoughts and being—dance, music, poetry, heart-to-heart conversation, a hobby, a life-long wish…
➤ Imagine a room of important, powerful, older people mocking the thing that expresses your inner thoughts and being.
➤ Imagine what it would be like if Jesus looked at something you did, said, painted, wrote, or thought, and then said to you, "It's perfect."
➤ Imagine a world where unique individuals were allowed to be themselves all the time with no fear of what others would think.

Move into the Bible study with comments like this—

Because there's so much pressure in today's world to be and look a certain way, people don't always feel comfortable showing their inner personalities. They might be afraid of being ridiculed, being rejected by friends, or being labeled in a negative way. But you cannot spend all your time living two different lives—one on the outside and another on the inside. There's a story in the Bible

You'll need—
- Bibles

about a woman who followed her heart and her instincts, even though it might have been embarrassing and strange in other peoples' eyes.

Have one or two students read Luke 7:36-50 aloud. Then discuss some of the following questions.

"I've learned that whatever I love to do, I do well."

—age 48

> ➤ The woman probably knew what the men at the Pharisee's house thought of her since she had led a sinful life. How might she have felt being in that room among them? Explain your thinking.
> ➤ The woman probably realized that the guests would think that her actions were outrageous and ridiculous. Why did she approach Jesus and pour the perfume on him anyway?
> ➤ In what ways did this woman show her inner self—the real her?
> ➤ Describe what it's like when all eyes are on you, watching, listening, and noticing everything.
> ➤ Describe what it's like when something you've created or been a part of is rejected by others.
> ➤ When is it most difficult to let the real you show? When you're with a certain person? In a group? At a certain place? During a particular circumstance? When is it easiest?

Close the session with something like this—

God created you as an individual. He is not in the business of creating robots who feel and behave only as he commands. He gives you a personality and a heart that defines who you are deep down inside, and then he lets you use that distinct personality and heart as you make choices along the way. The person you are on the inside is a person worth getting to know. God already knows her perfectly. You should too.

closing
Takin' It to Heart

In groups of two or three, let the girls share something meaningful about themselves that most people don't know. Then they can pray for one another, asking God to help them be brave enough to be who they really are.

Hand out copies of **On the Home Front** (page 29) as girls leave.

You'll need—
- Copies of **On the Home Front** (page 29), one for each student

All handouts are posted at
www.YouthSpecialties.com/store/girls
in plain text, Rich Text Format,
MS Word 95/6.0, and PDF formats.
Buyers of *Girls* can use them for *free!*

I'm All About

Circle 15 items that are most important to you.

achievements

family

grades

athletics

honesty

beauty

insightfulness

God/Jesus

kindness/serving

friends

bravery/courage

good health/well-being

church

marriage/family

creativity/music/
art/drama/writing

recognition/fame

self-esteem

social justice

WISDOM/KNOWLEDGE

boyfriends

ecology/nature/conservation

education

money

SEXUAL PURITY

success

10 Years Down the Road

How can a young woman find her true place in life? Is there any way she can discover what God really wants her to be and do? Almost every young woman hopes that her future holds some splendid purpose.

But you might feel like a plain, everyday sort of person who could never have an exciting and splendid life. How can there be something wonderful in my future? And if there is, how can I possibly figure out what it is?

The answer is simple: already during your past from time to time, God himself has whispered into your heart just that very wonderful thing, whatever it is, that he is wishing you to be and to do and to have. And that wonderful thing is nothing less than what's called your heart's desire. Nothing less than that. The most secret, sacred wish that lies deep down at the bottom of your heart, the wonderful thing that you hardly dare to look at, or to think about—the thing that you would rather die than have anyone else know of, because it seems so far beyond anything that you are or have at the present time, that you fear that you would be cruelly ridiculed if the mere thought of it were known—that is just the very thing that God is wishing you to do or to be for him.

And the birth of that marvelous wish in your soul—the dawning of that secret dream—was the Voice of God himself telling you to arise and come up higher because he had need of you.

Adapted from *Your Heart's Desire* by Emmet Fox (DeVorss Publications, 1933).

Think about your heart's desire—not the one about the cute guy who sits across from you in Algebra—the one about who you want to be and what you want to do. Maybe you've never told anyone about it. Maybe you've only written about it in your journal. Take the time to write out your heart's desire below. It can be one thing or a whole list of things.

heart's desires go here

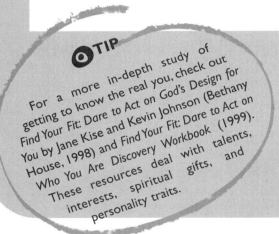

TIP

For a more in-depth study of getting to know the real you, check out *Find Your Fit: Dare to Act on God's Design for You* by Jane Kise and Kevin Johnson (Bethany House, 1998) and *Find Your Fit: Dare to Act on Who You Are Discovery Workbook* (1999). These resources deal with talents, interests, spiritual gifts, and personality traits.

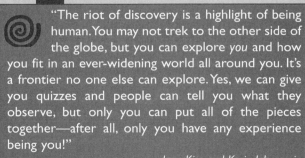

quote

"The riot of discovery is a highlight of being human. You may not trek to the other side of the globe, but you can explore *you* and how you fit in an ever-widening world all around you. It's a frontier no one else can explore. Yes, we can give you quizzes and people can tell you what they observe, but only you can put all of the pieces together—after all, only you have any experience being you!"

—*Jane Kise and Kevin Johnson in Find Your Fit (Bethany House, 1998, page 200)*

quote

"Big satisfaction comes from doing what God made you to do."

—*Kevin Johnson in What Do Ya Know? (Bethany House, 2000, page 12)*

Read the story of the woman who poured perfume on Jesus' feet in Luke 7:36-50. Think or journal about—

• A time you expressed the *real you* and it was accepted, praised, or encouraged.

• A time you expressed the *real you* and it was ridiculed, laughed at, or rejected.

• What Jesus sees when he looks at the *real you.*

——— PRAYER ———
Put Your Hands Together

God, it can be hard letting people see the real me. It feels safer to keep that person hidden inside, where no one can judge or ridicule or laugh. Help me see myself as you do, and help me recognize what's truly important to me. Teach me how to use the real me for you, no matter where I am or what I'm doing. Amen.

——— THOUGHT ———
For Your Gray Matter

Being a little-known *real* person is far superior to being a well-known *fake* person.

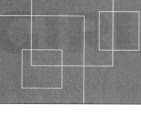

3 Your *Intrinsic* Self
On being knit by God

⬤ THE ISSUE

Most young women today have several different selves, not because they can't decide which one is real, but because they receive so many mixed messages. As important as it is for them to claim their own identity, regardless of the world's views, it's critical that they claim their God-given identity—daughter of the King.

---

introduction
Delvin' In

Now that your students have had a chance to look at how the world defines them and how they define themselves, it's time to look at the one true source of each person's identity—God himself. Everyone, of course, is created and loved by God equally. But for those who have chosen to be in relationship with him—Christians—"created and loved by God" takes on added meaning. God's part of the relationship doesn't change, as we all know. But how about the individual's part? Is any Christian now more important than a person who is not a Christian? More loved? More likely to succeed? More likely to live to a ripe old age without any problems?

Hardly. The change occurs when that person realizes who she *really* is. With that realization, the person is able to recognize herself as a child of God. She can look forward to an eternity with Christ—even on the worst days. And she can begin brushing aside the world's false views of her worth and success.

Many, maybe even all, of your girls may consider themselves to be Christians. They probably are. But do they realize the implications of that? A good number of mature adults don't even realize the implications. What was an

obvious and simple thing to believe as a small child—"God is my daddy"—becomes increasingly difficult as a girl grows up in this pressure-filled society. This session will give them a glimpse of the glorious life that is theirs because of their relationship with Christ.

quote

"The nicest thing we can do for our heavenly Father is to be one of his children."
—*St. Teresa of Avila*

Take some time this week to immerse yourself in Psalm 139. Read and reread the Bible verses found throughout this chapter. For you to help your students grasp their God-given identity, you must have a grasp of it yourself.

opening activity
Warmin' Up

option [for large groups]
Getting to Know You

If you have a group of 15 or more, move any chairs out of the way and have the girls stand in the middle of the room. Explain the game to them this way—

I'm going to call out specific descriptions, facts, or character traits of people. As soon as I do, it's your job

---

Live out this God-created identity the way our Father lives toward us, generously and graciously, even when we're at our worst. Our Father is kind; you be kind.
—*from Luke 6,* The Message

to group up with similar people. For example, if I call out eye color, you need to find everyone who has the same eye color as you as fast as possible. Stay in a group until I call out the next description.

If all goes well—and doesn't it always in youth ministry?—there will be a lot of energetic shouting as the extroverts in your group scream out, "Blue eyes! Blue eyes! All the blue eyes over here by me, *right now*!"

Here's a list of characteristics for you to call out. Add your own, too.

eye color	birth order (only, 1st, 2nd)
shoe size	introvert/extrovert
birth month	athlete/brainiac
number of siblings	social butterfly/other
year in high school	

After you have finished, ask for volunteers to name each person who was in one of their groups. (Name one that had quite a few girls in it.) If you have someone who can do that, ask for another volunteer to name the people in another group. Continue until the girls can see they've remembered very little of the factual information that was made known.

option [for small groups]
Getting to Know You

If you have 14 or fewer girls, have your teens pair up. If you have an odd number, partner with one of the gals yourself. Explain the game to them this way—

I'm going to give you one minute to find out as many vital facts about your partner as possible. You might ask for birthdate, shoe size, toothbrush color, favorite movie, hero, family members, favorite school subject, and so on. When I say, "Switch," the fact-gatherer becomes

the fact-giver and fact-giver becomes the fact-gatherer. Pay attention because when the two minutes are up, we're going to see how much you can each remember about your partner.

After the girls have finished gathering the data, ask for volunteers to share their mental lists.

exploring the topic
Diggin' a Little Deeper

Move into the next section with thoughts like these—

It's almost impossible to find out much about a person in the little time we've spent. You can gather a few facts, but they don't tell you much about the real person. Imagine if you had to remember one minute's worth of

> Hosea put it well: "I'll call nobodies and make them somebodies; I'll call the unloved and make them beloved. In the place where they yelled out, 'You're nobody!' they're calling you 'God's living children.'" Isaiah maintained this same emphasis:…"God doesn't count us; he calls us by name."
> —*from Romans 9, The Message*

information about everyone in this room—or everyone in this church, everyone in this town, everyone in this state, or everyone in the United States. Just keeping track of one minute's worth of facts would be far beyond impossible.

Think about this: God knows a complete lifetime worth of facts about every single person on the planet right now, every single person from the past, and every single person in the future. Some people might feel insignificant because of that. "I'm just one more person that God keeps catalogued in his file." But that's not true at all. The only possible reason that God would ever hold all that information in his heart would be because he deeply loves each and every one of us.

Choose one or more of the following activities.

option [group activity]
Daughter of the King

Choose one person to be the white-board keeper-of-the-list. Have that girl make three columns on the board with these titles—

You'll need—
- **Whiteboard**
- **Markers**
- **1 copy of Daughter of the King** (page 36)

➤ WHO I AM
➤ WHO GOD IS
➤ WHAT GOD DOES

Explain that you're going to read some verses from the Bible that talk about each person's identity as God defines it. Use the verses from **Daughter of the King** (page 36). After each verse, ask them for the following—

➤ How does God define you?
➤ How does God define himself?
➤ What does God do to you or for you?

> It's in Christ that we find out who we are and what we are living for. Long before we first heard of Christ and got our hopes up, he had his eye on us, had designs on us for glorious living, part of the overall purpose he is working out in everything and everyone.
> —*from Ephesians 1*, The Message

For example, after reading the verse from Galatians 3, students might answer, "God defines me as a child of God and an heir. He defines himself as my Father, and my Daddy. He adopts me." The keeper-of-the board needs only to write the key words in the appropriate columns.

After finishing all the verses, ask these questions—

➤ In what ways do you feel like God's child? Talk about that.

➤ If we are heirs of God, what might we inherit while we're still living on earth? Explain.
➤ If anyone here has ever felt like a nobody, describe what it's like when someone finally considers you a somebody.

option [video activity]
Simon Birch

Simon Birch and Joe have just been caught breaking in to the swimming coach's office, looking for clues to Joe's father's identity. Their friend, Ben, picks them up from the police station and the three of them talk about life and destiny by the lake at night. Show the clip.

You'll need—
- *Simon Birch*
- **TV and VCR**

0:58:49 Ben, Joe, and Simon walk out of the police station.
1:01:38 Simon says "I don't think so." Joe throws a rock into the lake.

Follow up with some questions like these—

➤ How does the world define people like Simon? Explain your thoughts.
➤ Do you think people who have unique circumstances like Simon are more aware of their spiritual identities? Why or why not?
➤ What prevents teen girls from believing they are God's beloved children? What prevents you from believing it?
➤ On a scale of one (I'm a freak!) to 10 (I'm a child of God, no doubt about it!) how confident do you feel about your God-given identity? Talk about that.

quote

"God loves me as a father loves his child. After all, He is my Father, the source of my being. He is the perfect father; His love for me is selfless."
—*Vincent P. Collins in* Me, Myself and You
(Abbey Press, 1974, page 166)

option [solo activity]
My Four Faces

Give each student a copy of **My Four Faces** (page 37) and a pen. Say something like—

You'll need—
• Copies of **My Four Faces** (page 37), one for each girl
• Pens

God doesn't only consider us his children. There are many other ways of describing our relationships with him. Look at the four listed on your handout.

> *parent-child*
> *potter-clay*
> *artist-painting*
> *lover-beloved*

For each of these examples, think about how and why God values you and what he does for you in that particular role. For example, when God is the artist, he might value you because he is pouring his soul into the painting, because he works hard to combine color and texture and shading to create something beautiful, and because when it's all done, he gets to sign his name on the bottom corner. What will he do for you as the painter? He will use only the finest paints, he will take his time to get each detail just right, and he will display you on his wall as one of his treasures.

You can tell for sure that you are now fully adopted as his own children because God sent the Spirit of his Son into our lives crying out, "Papa! Father!" Doesn't that privilege of intimate conversation with God make it plain that you are not a slave, but a child? And if you are a child, you're also an heir, with complete access to the inheritance.
—*from Galatians 4,* The Message

Give them several minutes to fill in the worksheet. If they seem unsure, consider pairing them up with another person. When they've finished, give them an opportunity to share their ideas with the group. Ask them some questions like these—

> If you could choose how God paints you, what would the painting look like? Why?
> If you could choose how God molds you, what would the sculpture look like? Why?
> If you could choose how God parents you, would he be more like a father or a mother? Talk about your ideas.
> What other ways can you describe your relationship with God? For example, teacher and pupil…

— Bible study —
Gettin' into the Word

The Angel Visits Mary
Luke 1:26-49

 Nudgers (nuj´erz) *n.* a tool used to gently push teens toward new insight

> Imagine receiving a personal visit from an angel.
> Imagine having a conversation with an angel.
> Imagine, at 14 or 15, being told the exact purpose for your life.
> Imagine being part of something humanly, scientifically, and theoretically impossible.
> Imagine being part of God's plan for the whole world.

After you've finished, transition into the next activity by saying—

Recognizing how God loves and defines us isn't easy. But then to actually believe it? That seems impossible at times. How could anyone—especially a perfect God— love us so much? The more you understand it though, the more your life will be changed. You will act different, feel different, and be different.

Mary, the mother of Jesus, is a perfect example. We're going to read part of her story.

Read Luke 1:26-49 to your group or have several students read it out loud. Then discuss the following—

- ➤ What do you think Mary was like?
- ➤ How do you think Mary changed after finding out what her purpose in life was?
- ➤ How would you respond if God told you that his plan for you might be dangerous? (In Mary's day, an unwed pregnant woman was punished by being stoned to death.)
- ➤ From this moment on, Mary's life was defined by one thing—her relationship to Jesus. What gives your life the most definition and direction?
- ➤ Do you agree or disagree with this statement: Some people have more important lives than others. Explain why you think so.

Close the session with comments like these—

It's good for you to recognize the ways the world defines you. That way you can fight against it. It's also good for you to recognize who you are deep down inside. That way you can look for

opportunities to nurture your dreams, values, and abilities. But most importantly of all, it's good for you to

What marvelous love the Father has extended to us! Just look at it—we're called children of God! That's who we really are. But that's also why the world doesn't recognize us or take us seriously, because it has no idea who he is or what he's up to. But friends, that's exactly who we are: children of God.
—*from 1 John 3,* The Message

recognize how God defines you—as his child, as his beloved, as the masterpiece he creates. You are, more than anything else, a product of God's creativity and awesome love.

closing

Takin' It to Heart

Have the girls close their eyes and think about their identity from God's perspective—how he values and loves them because he created them. While their eyes are still closed, have them take turns sharing what they're thankful for regarding their real identity, including new or personally challenging ideas from the lesson. These can be framed as statements ("I've learned that God cares about what I'm doing, even if it seems unimportant") or as short prayers ("Thanks, God, that you genuinely care about what I'm doing, every second of every day"). Hand out **On the Home Front** (page 38) as girls leave.

You'll need—

- Copies of **On the Home Front** (page 38), one for each student

All handouts are posted at www.YouthSpecialties.com/store/downloads
password: women
in plain text, Rich Text Format, MS Word 95/6.0, and PDF formats.
Buyers of *Girls* can use them for *free!*

Daughter of the King

Use the verses below to complete the activity on page 33. After reading each verse, ask these questions:

• How does God define you?

• How does God define himself?

• What does God do to you or for you?

Live out this God-created identity the way our Father lives toward us, generously and graciously, even when we're at our worst. Our Father is kind; you be kind.
—*from Luke 6,* The Message

Hosea put it well: "I'll call nobodies and make them somebodies; I'll call the unloved and make them beloved. In the place where they yelled out, 'You're nobody!' they're calling you 'God's living children.'" Isaiah maintained this same emphasis: . . . "God doesn't count us; he calls us by name."
—*from Romans 9,* The Message

You can tell for sure that you are now fully adopted as his own children because God sent the Spirit of his Son into our lives crying out, "Papa! Father!" Doesn't that privilege of intimate conversation with God make it plain that you are not a slave, but a child? And if you are a child, you're also an heir, with complete access to the inheritance.
—*from Galatians 4,* The Message

It's in Christ that we find out who we are and what we are living for. Long before we first heard of Christ and got our hopes up, he had his eye on us, had designs on us for glorious living, part of the overall purpose he is working out in everything and everyone.
—*from Ephesians 1,* The Message

What marvelous love the Father has extended to us! Just look at it—we're called children of God! That's who we really are. But that's also why the world doesn't recognize us or take us seriously, because it has no idea who he is or what he's up to. But friends, that's exactly who we are: children of God.
—*from 1 John 3,* The Message

My Four Faces

Think about each pair printed below. List some ways that you and God might fit those roles.

God as the parent | **Me as the child**

God as the potter | **Me as the clay**

God as the artist | **Me as the painting**

God as the creator | **Me as the creation**

On the Home Front

Read the story of Mary being visited by the angel in Luke 1:26-49. Think or journal about the following—

I have felt God telling or encouraging me to do something (describe when and what).

What does it mean for me to be God's child?

PRAYER
Put Your Hands Together

God, Father, Daddy,
Help me never forget who I am in your eyes. If I can keep that in mind, I'll be able to live the way you want me to. And I'll be more likely to become the me that you intend. Thank you for giving me such an awesome identity. Amen.

THOUGHT
For Your Gray Matter

Don't let your identity as God's child affect *parts* of your life; let it affect *all* of your life.

4 Reach for the Stars
Can *not*! Can *too*!

⬤ THE ISSUE

In the last 100 years, women have joined the voting ranks, entered the workplace, held high political offices, and been CEOs of major corporations. So why do young women still sense an invisible barrier they can't pass beyond? What is God's view on a young woman's potential and limitations?

---

introduction
Delvin' In

The concept of adolescence is fairly new to the human experience. It wasn't until after World War II, when high school became an experience for all youth, that *teenagers* appeared. Of course, people that age had always been around. But now,

---

quote

"Religion, especially when it promises direct contact with God, has often been a powerful vehicle of expressions for women.
Christianity may be patriarchal, but it declares that both sexes are equal in heaven. A religious movement like the Great Awakening, which was critical of things as they were, offered an opportunity for women to exercise a measure of independence and of leadership. Young men had plenty of opportunities to get out of the house and test their competence. The church was almost the only public institution to give females an important role."

— *Thomas Hine in* The Rise and Fall of the American Teenager
(Avon, 1999, pages 82-83)

---

their daily existence was being redefined. New limits were put on teens in terms of employment, independence, and how they spent their time. New opportunities were made available by way of education, athletic events, and fine arts.

The emotional wrangling that most teens began experiencing back then ("I'm old enough to work, but I have to go to school. I'm ready to run the farm, but I have to go to school. I thought I'd be settled down by now, but I have to go to school.") is still experienced to some extent by today's teens. Their bodies tell them they're adults. But the requirement of high school tells them they are not.

For girls, this struggle is twofold. Like young men, it involves the three-way tension between physical maturity, social maturity, and school. But young women also struggle with the tension between female potential and female limits.

This session is not attempting to debate women's roles in the church, family, workplace, and society. Even within the Christian community, there are many different viewpoints about women's roles. Rather, this session gives your young women a chance to express what they believe to be their limits and potential as indicated by the Bible, the church, their families, their teachers, the media, and other people in their lives.

Giving them a chance to discuss this issue will provide you an opportunity to see inside their hearts. Listen carefully, and by listening, try to understand the daily tensions they live with.

---

opening activity
Warmin' Up

Mission: Inconceivable

Before you begin, place all of the listed materials in the middle of the room. Gather your students together. Explain that

You'll need—
• Paper
• Pens
• Balloons
• Cans of soda
• Calculators

they are going to perform a series of simple acts, but there are specific guidelines to follow. Choose from the list below or make up your own. Don't spend too long on any single challenge.

- ➤ You must travel across the full width of the room, but you may not use your feet.
- ➤ You must take off your shoes and then put them back on the way they were, but you may not use either hand.
- ➤ You must blow up and tie off a balloon, but you may only use one hand.
- ➤ You must write your name on a piece of paper, but you may not use your dominant hand.
- ➤ You must open a can of soda, but you may not use both hands (yes, you can drink it, too).
- ➤ You must multiply 347 times 31, but you may not use your hands or your feet.

When you've finished, say something like—

Great job! I especially enjoyed watching you try to tie your shoes with one hand. There have probably been many times when you've felt frustrated or limited because something is preventing you from accomplishing what you set out to do.

In Christ's family there can be no division into Jew and non-Jew, slave and free, male and female. Among us you are all equal. That is, we are all in a common relationship with Jesus Christ.
—*from Galatians 3,* The Message

Then ask your students the following questions—

- ➤ What was the most frustrating or challenging task?
- ➤ What was the most ridiculous task?
- ➤ How does it feel to be limited in your actions? Explain.
- ➤ Give an example of another time when you were limited in performing an activity.

Diggin' a Little Deeper

Move on to the next section with something like this—

Most of you are fortunate enough to know how special you are in God's eyes. He loves you deeply and has great plans for your life. There are no limits to what God can do. But there are limits to what you can do, to what I can do—to what everybody in the world can do. Let's try to find out what limits are placed on us, and then talk about what your potential is as young Christian women in the world.

Choose one or more of the following activities.

option [group activity]
Would I? Could I? Should I?

Before the teens arrive, put one heading on each piece of paper: PARENTS, FRIENDS, TEACHERS, MYSELF, THE WORLD, and GOD. Underneath each heading, make three columns labeled GREEN LIGHT, YELLOW LIGHT, and RED LIGHT. You can write out the words or draw a traffic light emphasizing the appropriate color. Tape the sheets to the walls or lay them on the floor around the room. Give each student a marker. Explain the activity like this—

You'll need—
- 6 large pieces of paper
- Tape
- Markers

Let's take a look at how our lives are a combination of limits and potential. Each sheet of paper represents a different group of people: parents, friends, teachers, yourself, the world/ our culture/the media, and God. The three columns—green, yellow and red—represent the different messages you get. Green is "Go for it!" Yellow is

"Go ahead and try, but don't say I didn't warn you." Red is "No way."

Now think of some things you'd like to do and put it in one of the columns based on the message given about it. For example, on the sheet labeled self, you might put "apply to work on the yearbook" under the green circle (you're telling yourself to go for it), "ask to be considered as editor of the yearbook" under the yellow circle (you're telling yourself to ask but not to be disappointed if it doesn't work out), and "sing a solo in front of my friends" (you're telling yourself you wouldn't do it in a million years) under the red circle. The three things don't need to be related.

quote

"Before she has completely left childhood behind," wrote Alexis De Tocqueville (19th century) of the American girl, "she already thinks for herself, speaks freely and acts on her own. All doings of the world are ever plain for her to see. Seldom does an American girl, whatever her age, suffer from shyness or childish ignorance. She, like the European girl, wants to please, but she knows exactly what it costs."

— *Thomas Hine in* The Rise and Fall of the American Teenager
(Avon, 1999, page 99)

The ideas can be general, like "try out for an athletic team," or specific like "try out for the diving team."

Each of the entities titling the papers encourage you in some things, discourage you in others, and seem not to care in others. You don't have to write something on every sheet. List ideas that apply to you. It's okay to discuss your ideas with other people.

Give the girls enough time to give some thought into their answers—but not long enough to disconnect. You're looking for that magic moment when they've gotten involved in the activity without getting tired of it.

⊙ TIP

The best way to encourage your students' involvement is to participate yourself, so take the time to go around the room and add your thoughts to each category. Be honest!

After the girls have finished (and some will probably be stumped on at least one or two), gather together and ask questions.

➤ Think about who encourages you the most. Describe your relationship with him or her.

➤ Sometimes people are direct with their advice. They plainly say, "Go for it," or "Just give up, kid." What are more subtle ways that people communicate encouragement and discouragement?

➤ Think about the goals that are most important to you. Do people generally encourage or discourage you to attain your goals? Talk about that.

➤ You can be anything you want to be; you can do whatever you set your mind to. Do you agree or disagree with that statement? Why do you think that?

➤ How do you think your gender affects the limits and potential others see in you? Explain.

option [video activity]
A League of Their Own

In *A League of Their Own,* two sisters—stay-at-home, work-on-the-farm girls—are

You'll need—
• *A League of Their Own*
• TV and VCR

given the chance to play professional baseball after being spotted by a scout at a local softball game. Show the clip.

0:06:29 Fans are cheering for the local team.
0:15:15 "I'm nothing here."

Follow up with some discussion. Use these questions to get started.

> What limits do you think these women felt living on a farm in the 1940s, during a war?
> Even when offered "male" jobs as professional baseball players, the scout still commented on beauty and looks. Do you think that still happens today—women are given opportunities but their physical appearance is still an issue? Talk about that.
> Do young women feel trapped by their circumstances like Kit? Why or why not?
> Does having limitless opportunities make women happier? Why or why not?
> What limits are you experiencing or do you expect to experience in the future?

option [solo activity]
The Circle of Life

Give each student a copy of **The Circle of Life** (page 46) and a pen. Explain the activity to them like this—

You'll need—
• Copies of **The Circle of Life** (page 46), one for each student
• Pens

The three circles on this handout are for three categories of hopes or goals for your life—but not material things, such as owning a nice car or having a good-paying job. Think of nonmaterial hopes and goals.

For example, in the Nice but Not Necessary circle you might write, "to someday travel through all of Europe." In the I Want circle, you might write, "to get accepted at Stanford University." And in the I Really Want circle, you might put, "to

be a doctor who works with people in underdeveloped countries."

Your answers may be as specific or general as you'd like them to be. And every answer is legitimate, whether you want to be a kindergarten teacher, wife and mom, research scientist, or manager of a pet store. Remember, our identity is based in Christ, not in where we work or what titles we hold.

Then Miriam the prophetess, Aaron's sister, took a tambourine in her hand, and all the women followed her, with tambourines and dancing.

—*Exodus 15:20*

Give the girls several minutes to fill in their answers. When they've finished, ask for several volunteers to share their answers. Then ask a few questions—

> Do your parents and friends know what your goals for the future are? If not, why? If so, what do they think of them?
> Is what you wrote in your I Really Want circle something that women are generally encouraged or discouraged from doing? Explain why you think so.
> What roadblocks do you think you'll face in trying to reach the goals listed in I Really Want?
> How is your faith in God part of those things you really want? Do you need faith in God to achieve them? To maintain them?

option [second solo option]
Glad to Be Me

Hand out a copy of **Glad to Be Me** (page 47) and a pen to each girl. Make sure they each have a Bible. Say something like this—

You'll need—
• Copies of **Glad to Be Me** (page 47), one for each girl
• Pens
• Bibles

Sometimes, young women wish they had the advantages of being guys. But the fact is, you are young women, and that's how you have to live your life. There are a lot of great reasons to be glad you're a woman, the most important one being that God made you that way. First, take just a minute or two to list what you don't like about being female.

Pause for a bit while they make a list.

Now think about what you do like about being a woman. God created men and women, and when he finished, he said creation was "very good." Here's your chance to think about the very good aspects of being a woman. When you're finished making the list of good aspects, finish the worksheet.

Give your teens a few minutes to make a second list. Gather together and let students share a few items from their lists.

Ask some follow-up questions.

- ➤ Why are some women are dissatisfied with their gender? Talk about that.
- ➤ How can you remind yourself that you are a very good part of creation in God's eyes?
- ➤ What did you find in Psalm 139 that reassured you of your potential as a creation of God?

Bible study
Gettin' into the Word

Ruth
Ruth 1-4

You'll need—

• 5 copies of **Ruth's Story**
(page 48)

 Nudgers (nuj´erz) *n.* a tool used to gently push teens toward new insight

- ➤ Imagine living among total strangers, except for one crabby and bitter old woman.
- ➤ Imagine having absolutely no prospects for improving your life.
- ➤ Imagine being part of a despised minority that was considered inferior and second-class.
- ➤ Imagine working all day, every day, just to have enough food to eat.
- ➤ Imagine never having anyone acknowledge your hard work, creativity, individuality.
- ➤ Imagine living like that, and then finally meeting someone who recognized your value and encouraged your potential.

After you've finished the Diggin' a Little Deeper activities, move into the Bible study with some words like this—

Young women today are often told that they can be and do anything they want. Their potential is unlimited. At the same time, there are some obvious and not-so-obvious limitations put on women. You may feel that you have fewer opportunities in your school than the guys do. At home, you may feel like there are different expectations for you than for your brothers. At work, it might seem like guys get treated better.

Or maybe not.

> **quote**
>
> "The male brain is set up to be intensely spatial, the female brain is not…The male brain is not set up to be verbal but the female is… The female brain is at work in more sections than the male *just about all the time*. It is on call in a way the male is not. To use an analogy: the male brain turns on, like a machine, to do its task, then turns off; the female brain is always on… This difference is a primary reason males are so "task-oriented," testing out as less able than females to do a number of different kinds of tasks at once, and why males react to interruptions in their thinking with more of a sense of invasion than females tend to and, combined with testosterone-based aggression, more forcefully."
> —*Michael Gurian in* The Wonder of Boys *(J. P. Tarcher, 1997)*

Some of the limitations put on women are legitimate—females are the ones who bear children, females tend to be more nurturing than males, females generally are more verbal than males (it's been estimated that women need to express tens-of-thousands more words than guys each day—imagine that), and females are wired in the womb to perform multiple tasks at once. That's why you can talk on the phone to your friend while you paint your toenails while you cram for your history test while you plan what you're going to wear to school tomorrow while you work on your jump shot (okay, maybe that's a

> There was also a prophetess, Anna, the daughter of Phanuel, of the tribe of Asher…she never left the temple but worshiped night and day, fasting and praying.
>
> —*Luke 2:36-37*

slight exaggeration) while guys can either watch TV or do their homework.

God designed guys and girls differently, and that means there are certain limitations on each of them. You probably can't bench as much as the captain of your school's wrestling team, but the captain of your wrestling team will never bear a child.

Rather than read the entire book of Ruth, an abridged version is presented through a drama script. You might want to summarize the background for your students.

Ruth was a woman with very little future potential. Her husband, who was a Jew, had died, and her father-in-law and brother-in-law had died also. This left three widows with no one to provide for them. When Naomi, Ruth's mother-in-law, decided to return to her own country of Judah, Ruth went with her even though Naomi protested and told Ruth to go home to her parents.

Ruth had almost nothing going for her. She was a young widow with no children.

She was living with a mother-in-law who, quite frankly, had become cranky and unpleasant. Worst of all, she was a Moabite. Moabites were descendants of a woman who had become pregnant by her own father (see Genesis 19:36). God restricted marriages to foreign women and didn't allow them to be part of Jewish worship (Deuteronomy 23:2-3).

Imagine what it must have been like for Ruth to move to Judah. Alone, despised, looked down on—she might have felt like her life had no meaning and no possible way of improving. But God never looks at lives like that. He always sees potential—within the limits.

Ask for four volunteers to take parts for reading **Ruth's Story** (page 48). It's a condensed version of the book of Ruth taken directly from the *New Living Translation*.

After you finish the reading, discuss it using questions like these—

> ➤ Think of a time when you felt out of place, disliked, and hopeless. What made you feel that way?
> ➤ Ruth, a member of a despised minority, a woman with no hope for a better future, and a woman considered by most to have no potential, ended up giving birth to a son named Obed, who had a son named Jesse, who had a son named David—King David in the Bible—an ancestor of Jesus. That's a major

> It wasn't so long ago that you were mired in that old stagnant life of sin. You let the world, which doesn't know the first thing about living, tell you how to live.
>
> —*from Ephesians 2*, The Message

Cinderella ending. Do you think life can be meaningful and happy even without a Cinderella ending? Explain.
> ➤ Can you accomplish things in your life that will matter to others and make a difference like Ruth did? Talk about that.

Then say something like—

We all have limits we have to live within. Some are rules given by God or parents or teachers or the government. Some are physical because of the way God created our bodies. Some are emotional and mental. But spiritually, we have no limits at all. We can continue to grow and mature in our faith—to become more and more Christlike—for as long as we live. And if that becomes your focus as you begin exploring your potential, you can be sure God will guide you toward complete fulfillment.

quote

"The very little engine looked up and saw the tears in the doll's eyes. And she thought of the good little boys and girls on the other side of the mountain who would not have any toys or good food unless she helped. Then she said, 'I think I can. I think I can. I think I can.' And she hitched herself to the little train."

—*Watty Piper in* The Little Engine That Could *(Grosset & Dunlap, 1978)*

Takin' It to Heart

Have the girls break off into pairs or trios and share one thing they do that gives their life meaning and direction

You'll need—
- Copies of **On the Home Front** (page 49), one for each student

and one thing that they hope will give meaning and direction in the future. For example, "Helping take care of my younger sister gives my life meaning now, and I'd like to work toward becoming a teacher because I'd love to help kids learn to read." Have them pray for each other as they begin thinking and planning about the future.

Distribute **On the Home Front** (page 49) as they leave.

The Circle of Life

The circles below are for you to list some hopes or goals you'd like to see happen some day. In the outer circle, list hopes or goals that would be nice but aren't really necessary for happiness. In the middle circle, list some hopes or goals that you want and that you're planning to pursue. And in the center circle, list some hopes or goals that you definitely want and are willing to pursue wholeheartedly.

Nice but not necessary

I want it

I really want it!

GLAD to Be Me

On the left side of this page, write a list of female limitations you *don't* like. Then on the right side, make a list of what you *do* like—maybe even advantages—about being female.

What I don't like	What I do like

Look up Psalm 139. Read it to yourself once or twice. Awesome, isn't it? Think about the ways this psalm reassures you of your value and potential in God's eyes. List a few of them here.

Ruth's Story

CHARACTERS
Narrator
Ruth
Naomi
Boaz
Foreman

NARRATOR: So Naomi returned from Moab, accompanied by her daughter-in-law Ruth, the young Moabite woman. They arrived in Bethlehem at the beginning of the barley harvest. Now there was a wealthy and influential man in Bethlehem named Boaz, a relative of Naomi's husband. One day Ruth said to Naomi—

RUTH: Let me go out into the fields to gather leftover grain.

NARRATOR: So Ruth went out to gather grain behind the harvesters, which was customary there. And as it happened, she found herself working in a field that belonged to Boaz. While she was there, Boaz arrived from Bethlehem and greeted the harvesters. Then Boaz asked his foreman—

BOAZ: Who's that girl over there?

FOREMAN: She's the young woman from Moab who came back with Naomi.

NARRATOR: Boaz went over to Ruth and said—

BOAZ: Listen, my daughter. Stay right here with us when you gather grain; don't go to any other fields. You will be safe here.

NARRATOR: Ruth fell at his feet and thanked him warmly.

RUTH: Why are you being so kind to me? I am only a foreigner.

BOAZ: Yes, I know. But I also know about the love and kindness you have shown your mother-in-law since the death of your husband. I've heard how you left your father and mother and your own land to live here among complete strangers. May the Lord, the God of Israel, under whose wings you have come to take refuge, reward you fully.

RUTH: I hope I continue to please you, sir.

NARRATOR: So Ruth gathered barley there all day. She worked alongside the women in Boaz's field and gathered grain with them until the end of the barley harvest. Then she worked with them through the wheat harvest, too. One day Naomi said to Ruth—

NAOMI: My daughter, it's time that I found a permanent home for you, so that you will be provided for.

RUTH: I will do everything you say.

NARRATOR: After following Naomi's advice, Ruth and Boaz fell in love and got married. Boaz took Ruth home to live with him. The Lord enabled her to become pregnant, and she gave birth to a son. And they named him Obed. He became the father of Jesse and the grandfather of David, who became the most-loved king of Israel.

Take time this week to read the entire story of Ruth. It's a short book in the Old Testament, one of two books in the Bible named after a woman. Think or journal about these questions—

• How will being female affect the way you make future decisions?

• If you plan on having a family, how do you see your life taking shape in terms of children, job, career, marriage, and ministry?

— MEMORY VERSE —
Keep This in Mind

All the days ordained for me were written in your book before one of them came to be.

—*Psalm 139:16*

— PRAYER —
Put Your Hands Together

Father, it's good to know that when you look at me, you see my potential. Help me to live an obedient life as I think about the future and begin exploring it. Guide me in my decisions. I know that I'll be happiest if I find the job or task you've designed me for. Thank you for giving my life definition by giving me the limitations you have. Amen.

— THOUGHT —
For Your Gray Matter

The people who acknowledge and accept their limitations are the people who have the most potential.

Reach for the Stars |

⊙ THE ISSUE

High school girls have no choice but to exist alongside high school guys. But since guys are obviously from another planet (umm…Mars, maybe?), that's not always easy. It helps if girls understand the way God designed guys.

---

introduction

You knew we'd get here eventually—the gender comparison session. Actually, this isn't so much about comparing genders as it is about trying to understand the other gender. And that's no easy task. But it's easy to ask, "Why did God have to make us so different?!" Listen to the frustrated cries of teen girls—

- ➤ Why won't guys just sit down and talk?
- ➤ What's the big deal about not crying in public?
- ➤ What's the big deal about not crying, period?
- ➤ Why do they stare at me like that?
- ➤ Why do they only ask out the beautiful girls?
- ➤ How can they sit and watch football for hours on end without getting bored?
- ➤ Why are they so immature?
- ➤ Do they really think it's cool to act like such a hot-shot?
- ➤ Do they really think it's cool to act so macho?
- ➤ Do they really think it's cool to be so vulgar?
- ➤ Et cetera

Yes, God certainly made men and women different. Which is a wonderful thing. And a terrible thing, especially for teenagers who, besides trying to understand the opposite sex, are also trying to understand themselves, the world, their parents, the future, and just about everything else.

The Bible doesn't explain many specifics about the differences between men and women, but it implies plenty. Men waged wars. Men fell prey to brazen women. Men lusted after women and found themselves in plenty of trouble. Men were judgmental of promiscuous women but not promiscuous men. In those days, men ran the show. (Thank goodness for Deborah and Esther and Mary.)

There are plenty of implications about women, too. They were often described as nags. Some were cynical disbelievers. Some were just as sexually corrupt as men (think back to Lot's daughters). In the Proverbs, less-than-pleasant women were referred to in a variety of ways—drippy faucets, rings in a pig's snout, quarrelsome, seductive, smooth-tongued.

Besides the Biblical implications, there are plenty of scientific studies that deal with gender differences, especially in the brain. A biggie is that the male brain is wired to be spatial; hence the popularity of blocks, Legos, and buildings sets among boys. The male brain is not wired to be as verbal. The male brain, while being almost 10 percent larger in size than the female brain, is used in fewer areas less often than the female brain, which has multiple areas at work and is on call almost nonstop. While most girls can juggle

⊕
The Lord God said, "It is not good for the man to be alone. I will make a helper suitable for him."

—*Genesis 2:18*

many tasks at once, most guys begin and end a single task at a time.

This session is about helping girls understand guys. For the development of this session, many

---

teen girls wrote down questions and observations about guys. Then guys tried to answer the questions and address the observations. This isn't a full-fledged manual on understanding guys, but it should help get the ball rolling.

Top Ten Ways Boys Are Different from Girls

Compiled by Linni Miller, age 4, Atlanta

1. Boys like to play with trucks more than girls.
2. Boys like to eat more than girls.
3. Boys like dinosaurs more than girls.
4. Boys are bigger than girls.
5. Boys have shorter hair than girls.
6. Boys don't wear dresses.
7. Boys don't wear their coats when it's cold outside.
8. Boys are taller than girls.
9. Boys can be daddies but girls can't.
10. Boys have tails.

Top Ten Ways Girls Are Different from Boys

Compiled by Austen Nelson, age 4, San Diego

1. Girls wear dresses.
2. Boys wear underwear; girls wear panties.
3. Girls leave the seat down.
4. Girls have long hair.
5. Girls don't play baseball.
6. Girls don't have pee-pees.
7. Daddies have hairy bodies.
8. Girls like dolls.
9. Mommies use make-up instead of shaving cream.
10. Girls scream; boys roar.
Bonus: Girls wear fingernail polish.

It took Linni Miller approximately five minutes to complete her list while sitting at the kitchen table neatly coloring a picture. It took Austen Nelson about four days, due to the fact that he'd previously devoted himself to a different task, namely playing with trucks, and when he finally reached number 4, he ran through the living room making engine noises and said, "Mom, can't you just do it for me?"

opening activity
Warmin' Up

Gender Outburst

Tell your students they're going to play a new edition of Outburst designed just for them. Ask for a volunteer to be scorekeeper and a volunteer to be the emcee. Explain the rules as follows—

You'll need—
- 2 copies of Gender Outburst (page 57)
- Pen for the scorekeeper
- Stopwatch or clock with a second hand

> ***When the game begins,*** *[insert the emcee's name]* ***is going to give you a topic. You have 30 seconds to yell out as many answers as you can think of.*** *[Insert the scorekeeper's name]* ***has a list of the top five answers for each topic. When you yell a correct one, she'll mark it off on the sheet and yell, "Yes," so you know you've scored a point. Remember, think quickly and yell loudly.***

Let the emcee know it's her job to give the group each new topic when they're ready and to keep track of the time. Let her know how long each round will last. Tell the scorekeeper to put a checkmark by each answer the group gets right and to yell, "Yes," so they know they've scored. Play as many rounds as you have time for, but stop *before* your teens get tired of it. When play is over, ask the following questions—

> ➤ Which of your answers are true and accurate, not just stereotypes? Explain why you think so.
> ➤ How did you come up with your answers? From school? From TV? From other girls? From first-hand observation? Something else?
> ➤ Without naming names, do you know any guy who fits all the stereotypes? Explain.
> ➤ How do your personal opinions and prejudices about guys and their stereotypes affect the way you think about guys? Communicate with guys? Relate to guys?

Make sure your students are clear about this: these are generalizations only. These are perceptions. These are opinions. Yes, there are guys who fit some of those criteria, but usually not all of them, all of the time.

exploring the topic

Diggin' a Little Deeper

Move into this section with something like this—

While it's true that guys and girls are different, and many of those differences are difficult to relate to, it's important that we don't put any more barriers between you and guys than are already there. It's wrong to assume that all guys are immature for their age just because you know one who is. It's wrong to assume that all guys have only one thing on their minds, even though it's true of some guys in your school. It's wrong to assume that all guys are emotionless, uncommunicating aliens, even if the guy who sits next to you in geometry is.

It feels pretty bad if we turn the tables: "All girls are gossips. All girls are on an emotional roller coaster. All girls are obsessed with their weight. All girls are ultra-crabby once a month."

Not a pretty picture. Guys don't like to be clumped into one category any more than girls do. Guys deserve to be understood and accepted for who they are—a species quite different from you.

quote

"Why are guys so competitive? It's just part of our nature. I *hate* losing. It's a guy thing."
—*a guy, quoted by Susie Shellenberger*
in Anybody Got a Clue About Guys? (Vine Books, 1995)

Choose one or more of the following options.

option [group activity]
Straight from the Horse's Mouth

Invite two or three guys to attend as your panel experts. They should be reasonably mature, clear communicators, honest, and the same age as or

You'll need—
- 2 or 3 guys (see directions for details)
- Slips of paper and pens—or questions written by your group members ahead of time

older than your girls. College students or young adults would be great. Their answers are likely to hold more weight with the girls due to their ages and life experiences. Be sure your panelists know beforehand that—

➤ They may get asked direct and probing questions.
➤ Some of the questions might be embarrassing.
➤ Some of the questions might seem ridiculous to them, but they should never indicate it.
➤ If a question hits too close to home, they have the right to pass on it.

When you begin the activity, tell your girls that the best way to understand guys is not to talk *about* them but to talk *to* them, asking them questions about how and why they're so different than girls.

Introduce your panel of experts to the group. Explain that they're available to answer whatever questions the girls may have about guys as well as they can.

There are two ways to do this. First, let the girls raise their hands and ask questions directly. If you think your group is confident enough to do this, it's an efficient way to go. A second way is to let the girls write single questions on pieces of paper anonymously. Then the panel reads and answers the questions one by one. This may encourage your girls to ask things they might be too embarrassed to ask otherwise, and it may help your panel feel less on-the-spot, especially if they know some of the girls personally.

> ◉ **TIP**
> **If circumstances allow, have your girls write questions a week or two ahead. You can read through them and remove inappropriate and duplicate questions before the activity begins.**

> ◉ **TIP**
> **If you choose this option, be sure you have all your students sign thank-you cards for the panelists at the end of the session (after they've left). Stamp them and put them in the mail *that night*. It's the least you can do for people who've gone out on a limb for you.**

option [video activity]

Grease

You need to act as emcee for the activity in the following ways—

- ➤ If a question is clearly inappropriate, simply say, "We'll pass on that one," without embarrassing the questioner.
- ➤ If your panelists tend to be long-winded, help them keep their answers to a reasonable length by turning to another panelist and asking for his thoughts.
- ➤ If girls are hesitating to ask questions, get the discussion moving by asking some questions of your own. Be prepared so there are no long, awkward silences. Here are some ideas—

  —Is it true that guys think it's weak to cry? Why?
  —Is locker room talk really as bad as people say it is? How does a guy keep from being involved in it without losing face with his friends?
  —If how a girl dresses affects a guy's thoughts, how can we make better choices about what we wear?
  —Besides outer appearance, what are things that guys admire most in a girl?
  —Is it possible for a guy and girl to just be good friends?

> Wise men and women are always learning, always listening for fresh insights.
>
> —*from Proverbs 18,* The Message

Show two scenes from *Grease*. The first scene shows the summer romance between Danny (John Travolta) and Sandy (Olivia Newton-John). This will help set up the second scene, in which Danny and Sandy relate tales of their summer romance—in completely different ways.

You'll need—
- *Grease*
- TV and VCR

0:00:00 The opening scene of *Grease*.
0:01:25 The summer romance scene fades.

0:13:50 The guys on the bleachers ask Danny about his summer romance.
0:17:48 The song ends with the phrase, "Tell me more."

Ask the following questions—

- ➤ What aspects of Sandy's story were the girls interested in hearing?
- ➤ What aspects of Danny's story were the guys interested in hearing?
- ➤ Was Danny relating events as he really experienced them or as he wanted his friends to think they happened? Why do you think so?
- ➤ How can two people view the exact same event in two totally different ways?
- ➤ Have you ever been in a situation where guys and girls had entirely different opinions, ideas, perspectives, and observations? Talk about that.

option [solo activity]

Can't Live with 'Em, Can't Live without 'Em

Hand out **Can't Live with 'Em, Can't Live without 'Em** (page 58) and a pen to each girl. Give them several minutes to

You'll need—
• Copies of **Can't Live with 'Em, Can't Live without 'Em** (page 58), one for each girl
• Pens

work on it. Then gather as a group. Ask some volunteers to share and explain their answers. Then ask some follow-up questions—

➤ How do your ratings affect the way you choose guy friends? The way you choose boyfriends?

➤ What are some ways you can work to be less annoyed by the differences between guys and girls?

➤ How do you want to be treated and thought of by guys? How might they want to be treated and thought of by you?

➤ Why do you think God designed these differences into guys and girls?

— Bible study —

Gettin' into the Word

Joseph and Mary
Luke 1:26-56, 2:15-19 and Matthew 1:18-25

Transition into the Bible study by saying—

You'll need—
• Bibles

There's no question about it—guys and girls are different. They've been different since the beginning of time. Even though God designed these differences to complement one

another, often they end up doing just the opposite—pitting the men against the women, females against the males, guys against the girls.

We're going to look at one couple in the Bible whose differences were very apparent to see what we can learn.

Ask for different volunteers to read the Bible verses at the appropriate time. Follow the outline below for your talk.

Nudgers (nuj´erz) n. a tool used to gently push teens toward new insight

➤ Mary and the angel had a conversation. They both spoke.
➤ When the angel spoke, Joseph listened.
➤ Mary's reaction to discovering she would be Jesus' mother? Find her cousin to tell her all about it.
➤ Mary's response was a song that deals with a little information and a lot of emotions.
➤ Joseph's initial response was a pragmatic plan for dealing with the sticky situation.
➤ Joseph's reaction to the angel? Simply follow the angel's instructions.
➤ Mary's reaction to the birth of her son? She stored all her thoughts and memories in her heart and thought about them.
➤ Joseph's reaction to the birth of his son? "He named him Jesus."

Have one student read Luke 1:26-38. When she is finished, ask a couple of questions.

➤ Do you think Mary's questions were a sign of disbelief and doubt, a sign of belief and wonder, or a sign of something else?

➤ Describe the meeting between Mary and the angel. How were they each involved?

God saw all that he had made, and it was very good.
—*Genesis 1:31*

Have another student read Matthew 1:18-21. Then ask more questions.

➤ Describe Joseph's meeting with the angel and his response to the message.

➤ How was this different from Mary's meeting and response?

Have another student read Luke 1:39-56. Follow up with questions after this passage.

> ➤ Describe Mary's actions after the angel left. In what ways were they uniquely female?

Have another student read Matthew 1:24. Then ask—

> ➤ Describe Joseph's actions after the angel left. In what ways were they uniquely male?

Have someone read Luke 2:15-19. Then say—

> ➤ Describe Mary's reaction to the birth of Jesus. In what way was it uniquely female?

Finally, have someone read Matthew 1:25. Follow up with—

> ➤ Describe Joseph's reaction to the birth of Jesus. In what way was it uniquely male?

Then finish up with something like this—

> *Mary and Joseph are just one example in the Bible of how men and women can view the same situation through completely different eyes. And it's not always the woman who is emotional and the man who is practical. David wept bitterly when one of his children died. Delilah was a cold and unfeeling woman. Women are not all the same. Men are not all the same. But men and women? They're almost never the same as each other. And that is by God's design. If Mary and Joseph had both been overcome with emotion, who would have taken care of business, like trying to find an inn or a stable to give birth in? Or if they'd both been practical observers, who would have bestowed caresses and hugs and love onto the newborn baby? Their differences made the situation stable and complete.*
>
> *Guys may be hard to understand. They may be annoying on occasion. They may be exasperating. But God made them "very good." God always knows what he's doing...even with guys. Trust him.*

---

closing

Takin' It to Heart

As you close, ask your girls to respond to one of the following—

You'll need—

- Copies of **On the Home Front** (page 59), one for each student

> ➤ something new I learned about guys
> ➤ something I used to think was true about guys but I don't after tonight
> ➤ something I've learned to appreciate about guys
> ➤ something I need to work on to understand and relate to guys better

Encourage every girl to share her response with the group. Then ask for volunteers to pray for—

> ➤ the guys in the youth group
> ➤ brothers
> ➤ fathers
> ➤ appreciation for the differences between men and women

As the students leave, give them copies of **On the Home Front** (page 59).

All handouts are posted at
www.YouthSpecialties.com/store/downloads
password: women
in plain text, Rich Text Format,
MS Word 95/6.0, and PDF formats.
Buyers of *Girls* can use them for *free!*

---

quote

 I've learned that you can't judge boys by the way they look."

—age 12

Gender Outburst

Give one copy of this sheet to the emcee to announce the topics and one copy to the scorekeeper to check off the correct answers.

1. Things some guys do when they eat

- O drink milk from a carton
- O stuff an entire hamburger in at once
- O put ketchup on everything
- O belch
- O call salad "rabbit food"

2. Things some guys do when they dress

- O let the top of their boxer shorts show
- O wear the same shirt day after day after day
- O mix clashing colors
- O leave their shirt hanging out
- O wear a T-shirt one day and a dress shirt the next

3. Things some guys don't do

- O carry on a conversation
- O talk about how they're feeling
- O remember important dates
- O notice that a girl has a new hairstyle
- O ask how someone else is feeling

4. Things some guys don't understand

- O girls
- O emotions
- O why girls go to the bathroom in groups
- O why girls get upset when guys say, "What's wrong?" and girls answer, "Nothing," and guys believe them
- O the importance of being on time for a date

5. Ways guys are portrayed in commercials–

- O tough cowboy
- O tough four-wheel-drive truck owner
- O zombie-football-watching-insensitive guy
- O crazy for a pretty face
- O pizza inhaler

6. Worst ways a guy can ask out a girl

- O over the phone
- O leave a message on her pager
- O send a note via a friend
- O through a mutual friend
- O over the Internet

7. Best ways a guy can ask out a girl

- O face to face, plus a nice card to read later
- O face to face, plus flowers
- O face to face, plus chocolate
- O face to face, plus a musical serenade
- O face to face, period

Read each of the following ideas. Mark how you feel about the topic on the scale under it.

Can't Live with 'Em, Can't Live without 'Em

When a guy makes a rude joke in my presence

can't stand it	bothers me sometimes	don't care about it	kinda like it	really like it
☐	☐	☐	☐	☐

When a guy asks for my opinion about a class assignment

can't stand it	bothers me sometimes	don't care about it	kinda like it	really like it
☐	☐	☐	☐	☐

When a guy asks me whether he thinks my best friend would go out with him

can't stand it	bothers me sometimes	don't care about it	kinda like it	really like it
☐	☐	☐	☐	☐

When a guy in my PE class treats me like I don't know anything about sports

can't stand it	bothers me sometimes	don't care about it	kinda like it	really like it
☐	☐	☐	☐	☐

When a guy ignores me when I try to talk to him

can't stand it	bothers me sometimes	don't care about it	kinda like it	really like it
☐	☐	☐	☐	☐

When a guy treats me like a buddy, not like a girl

can't stand it	bothers me sometimes	don't care about it	kinda like it	really like it
☐	☐	☐	☐	☐

When a guy eats like a slob in front of me

can't stand it	bothers me sometimes	don't care about it	kinda like it	really like it
☐	☐	☐	☐	☐

When a guy doesn't acknowledge my presence

can't stand it	bothers me sometimes	don't care about it	kinda like it	really like it
☐	☐	☐	☐	☐

When a guy I'm a friend with outside of school pretends like he doesn't know me at school

can't stand it	bothers me sometimes	don't care about it	kinda like it	really like it
☐	☐	☐	☐	☐

When a guy assumes I can't do something because I'm a girl

can't stand it	bothers me sometimes	don't care about it	kinda like it	really like it
☐	☐	☐	☐	☐

This week, think about how differently Mary and Joseph reacted to the angels, the pregnancy, and the birth. Spend some time thinking or journaling about the following—

• The different roles of girls and guys, men and women

• Ways that the differences between guys and girls have a positive impact on relationships, families, and the world

So God created people in his own image; God patterned them after himself; male and female he created them.

—*Genesis 1:27, NLT*

PRAYER
Put Your Hands Together

God, I am so glad that you made both men and women. I don't always understand guys. I don't even always like guys. But I know that you intentionally created them uniquely and wonderful. Help me to recognize the differences between men and women, and help me to appreciate those differences instead of getting frustrated over them. Amen.

THOUGHT
For Your Gray Matter

God created men and women differently for the very same reason that he created you and me differently—because he loves variety, uniqueness, and individuality.

Dating and Sexuality

6

Everything you've ever wanted to know that can fit into one session

THE ISSUE

For many teens, the subjects of sexuality and dating are in-your-face topics. Unfortunately, they're getting most of their information from the entertainment industry and their peers. It's time to reverse that trend and show teens that the church is ready to talk about these two issues in a biblically truthful and culturally relevant way.

introduction

Delvin' In

Ah, at last. The session that many of your girls have been waiting for with bated breath. And why not? After all, the attraction they feel for the opposite sex is natural, God-designed, and good. But the attraction is not the only issue. The actions that often result from that attraction are equally—if not more—important.

Today's teens, more than any other generation, are in what must feel like an impossible situation. While their bodies are

> **quote**
>
> Repeat after me: 'I will *never* play dumb just to get a guy's attention.' If you do, you're in worse shape than the guy is."
>
> —*Susie Shellenberger in*
> *Anybody Got a Clue About Guys? (Vine Books, 1995)*

nearing maturity, their days are being spent in the classroom. While they're intellectually deciding to wait for marriage until they've attended college and settled into a career, their bodies are physically saying, "No way!" While parents, educators, and ministry leaders are telling them to wait-wait-wait, their hormones are saying, "As if," "Yeah, right," "I don't think so."

The parents, educators, and ministry leaders are decidedly right. God is clear that sexual activity is to be reserved for marriage. But teens' hormones are God's creation. Their bodies were designed to feel attracted to the opposite sex. At the intersection of these teenage crises, there is a major head-on collision waiting to happen.

Wham! Crash and burn!

There is nothing you can do to erase the reality of your students' hormones. Nor can you reverse the *trend* of marriage beyond the teen years. Never mind that up until 75 or 100 years ago, most of your students would already be married. This is the 21st century, an age where marriage comes later, hormones come when they will, the world says "have safe sex," and the church says, "No sex until you've said, 'I do.'" What a predicament.

There are several current philosophies in the Christian culture about dating. The first is to give up the institution of dating as outlined in the best-selling *I Kissed Dating Goodbye*. The second is to participate in the dating world, but within God's guidelines, and there are plenty of books instructing kids how to do that. God's guidelines for dating, unfortunately, are not so clearly spelled out in the Bible. While there are clear references to sex, courtship, and marriage, there is nothing on dating. No ideas for great dates. No rules for exactly what to say, what to wear, and what to do.

But this session is going to take a stab at uncovering some important principles. Hang on

> **TIP**
> You may want to copy and mail the parent letter found on page 73. (Or adapt it to your situation.) Give them an opportunity to call you with suggestions or concerns.

for the ride. With God's direction and guidance, everyone should come out in one piece.

⊙ TIP

If you're working with older teens and you and your girls want to pursue this topic in more detail, check out *Good Sex: A Whole-Person Approach to Teenage Sexuality & God* by Jim Hancock and Kara Eckmann Powell (Youth Specialties, 2001).

— opening activity —

Warmin' Up

Whose Dating Line Is It Anyway?

This activity will be great fun *if* you gear it to your specific group. If you have a lot of introverts, let them set the pace and the tone of the game. Don't push them too far, and

> **You'll need—**
>
> - 1 copy of **Whose Dating Line Is It Anyway?** (page 67)
> - Props such as a telephone, a steering wheel, a football jersey or letterman jacket, pom-poms, studious-looking glasses, textbooks, plastic or silk flowers

don't force them into working either alone or in a pair. Let them choose which they prefer. If you have a lot of extroverts, sit back and enjoy the entertainment.

Use the scenarios on **Whose Dating Line Is It Anyway?** (page 67). For each scenario, there is an example you can give to jumpstart your students' thinking.

Explain the game to your students—

I'll describe a situation. It's your job to come up with a word, phrase, or sentence that fits. For example, if the card says, "Worst thing you can say on a date when he asks where you want to eat" you could give the following lines—

- *Burger King. That's probably all you can afford, right?*

- *I don't know. Where do you want to go?*
- *Any place with a salad bar. I'm watching my weight.*

I'll call out one or more names. You'll come up, pick a prop if you'd like, and deliver your line. There aren't right or wrong lines. Just have fun and be creative.

Call on several students to perform for each card. It usually takes at least one or two students to get the enthusiasm rolling. Keep things moving quickly. No lag time allowed. When you're done, vote on the funniest, the most likely to actually happen, and the least likely to actually happen. Have fun!

— exploring the topic —

Diggin' a Little Deeper

⊙ TIP

Be aware of the fact that some of your girls have never been on a date before. Make sure this session doesn't sound like a how-to-date-the-right-way pep talk. Instead it should be a when-I-start-dating-these-are-some-things-for-me-to-consider. That way, no one will feel like less than the amazing and wonderful person God made her.

Move into the next section by saying something like this—

It's easy—and pretty hilarious—to imagine all the embarrassing and funny things that might happen on a date. Until one of them actually happens, of course. This thing we call the dating game isn't really a game at all. It's a serious thing, so it's worth thinking about before jumping in head first.

- ➤ What might God think about dating? Why do you think that?
- ➤ Can you think of any stories from the Bible that might relate to the issue of dating? What are they?
- ➤ Is it ever okay for a Christian to go out with a non-Christian? Why or why not?
- ➤ What are your parents' guidelines for dating? What do you think about them?

Choose one or more of the following activities.

option [group activity]
National Weather Service Brainstorm Warning

Before you begin, make two columns on the whiteboard. Title one DATING PROS and the other DATING CONS.

You'll need—
- Whiteboard
- Markers

Ask for a volunteer to be the whiteboard CEO and write down key words of the brainstorming ideas.

Explain to your group that there are many different ways to view dating. Begin with the Dating Pros and ask for ideas about the positive aspects of dating. For example, "Dating provides an opportunity to learn how to communicate with guys better."

After you have a list of positive ideas, move to Dating Cons. An example of this is, "Dating can put people in an awkward situation if they don't both have the same morals." Push your girls to think beyond the simple answers. The cons of dating may present real-life issues for at least some of your girls.

Now's your chance to provide some positive input that can counter all the ridiculous ideas about dating that are floating around in magazines and on TV. After finishing the two lists, ask your girls to brainstorm ideas for creative dates. You don't have to write these down, though you may want to keep a record of them for your own files. When you've finished, ask the following questions or some of your own—

Then say something like—

Some Christians think dating isn't a good idea. Others think it's okay as long as there are clear boundaries. God doesn't give us clear-cut instructions: "Thou shalt not date" or "Thou shalt date but only if he is one year older than you, two inches taller than you, attends a mid-week Bible study, and first calls your father to ask permission." Which means that we're left to decide for ourselves how dating fits into our relationship with God.

option [video activity]
Back in the Saddle Again

After his wife has been dead for about a year, Sam (Tom Hanks) finally gets up the

You'll need—
- *Sleepless in Seattle*
- TV and VCR

nerve to get "back in the saddle again" and ask out a woman. Show the clip.

0:42:45 Right after Sam walks down the stairs and the music starts.

0:44:30 Sam sits down and the music ends.

Ask questions like this—

> ➤ Do you think it's really that nerve-wracking for guys to ask out girls? Explain.

> ➤ Would you ever call a guy to ask him out? Why or why not?

quote

"Doyouwanttogoonadate?"
"What?"
"Doyouwanttogoonadate?"
"What?"
"Doyouwanttogoona—who is this? Oh, I have the wrong number."
—*from* Teenage Romance *(Delia Ephron, Viking, 1981)*

option [solo activity]
Date Sale

Hand out a copy of **Date Sale** (page 68) and a pen to each girl. Go over the directions on the top of the sheet with them. Give them several minutes to do their shopping. Regather as a group and ask each girl (if you have time, otherwise ask for volunteers) to read her finished shopping list. Then ask questions—

You'll need—
• Copies of **Date Sale** (page 68), one for each girl
• Pens

> ➤ What did you base your shopping choices on?
> ➤ In what ways was this shopping spree like real life?
> ➤ If a guy were to ask you out, what criteria would you use to decide whether you'd go? (Encourage your girls to move beyond, "Whether or not I like him.")
> ➤ In our community is it okay for girls to ask guys out? What do you think? Explain your answers.

> ➤ If you were interested in dating a certain guy, would you consider asking him out?

┌─ Bible study ─────────────────
Gettin' into the Word
└───────────────────────────────

The Spirit of the Law
Selected verses

This Bible study is different from the others since it doesn't relate truth based on a story. Instead, you and your students are going to take some time to think about and discuss only a few verses.

You'll need—
• Copies of **Heart and Soul** (page 69), one for each girl
• Copies of **Recipe for Peace in Your Dating Life** (pages 70-71), one for each girl
• Pens
• Bibles

Move into the Bible study with something like this—

Most teenagers have a lot of questions about dating and sexuality. Teens who aren't believers probably get most of their information, guidelines, and instruction from the media—TV, magazines, and movies. But where can a Christian—knowing that the media's message isn't entirely true or accurate—go for answers? The Bible leaves a lot of blanks in terms of dating and sexuality. The Bible makes two principles exceedingly clear—

Jacob was in love with Rachel and said [to her father], "I'll work for you seven years in return for your younger daughter Rachel." So Jacob served seven years to get Rachel, but they seemed like only a few days to him because of his love for her.
—*Genesis 29:18, 20*

• *People who are dating must respect one another in every possible way.*
• *Sexual intercourse before marriage is a sin.*

But that leaves a lot to figure out, doesn't it? We're going to look at a few verses in the Bible to see if we can't come up with some guidelines for healthy sexuality and dating. Then we'll look at some great advice from a guy who knows what's what with dating, sexuality, and teenagers.

Hand out **Heart and Soul** (page 69) and pens to all the girls. Work on this activity as a group. It's a great opportunity for you to listen to your students' insights, concerns, fears, questions, and confusion about dating and sexuality.

◑ TIP
This topic will be addressed again from a different viewpoint in the next session, "Blessed Are the Pure in Heart."

Have one student read the first set of verses listed on the handout. If other translations are available, let your students read from those also.

Facilitate honest and open discussion with the following questions. Be confident. This *is* a topic they want to talk about.

➤ How does God want you to view your body?
➤ What messages do you get from the media about how to view your body?
➤ Why do you think talking about, reading about, watching movies about, and actually participating in sex are so prevalent among high schoolers?
➤ What might change that trend?
➤ What do you think prevents so many people from treating their bodies with dignity?

Ask another student to read the second passage of Scripture. Read it from other translations you might have. Discuss questions like the following—

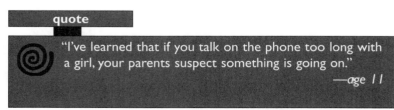
"I've learned that if you talk on the phone too long with a girl, your parents suspect something is going on."
—*age 11*

➤ These verses say we should concentrate on pleasing God. Who do you think teens in general try to please the most? Talk about that. Who do you—honestly—try to please the most? Talk about that.
➤ Pleasing God isn't supposed to be a dreadful event. As Paul writes in *The Message*, it's supposed to be a "living, spirited dance." What does that mean? How can you pursue that?
➤ What's your parents' definition of sexual promiscuity? Your church's definition? Your friends' definition? Yours?
➤ God describes humans as being both body and soul, both mind and spirit. We aren't made of only physical or emotional or intellectual parts, but rather all three. What implications does that have for people who have sex before being married? Explain your thinking.
➤ What can you do to prevent yourself from engaging in sexually promiscuous activity? (It won't happen by itself. You must have a plan.)

✚
The Lord God said, "It is not good for the man to be alone."
—*Genesis 2:18*

After discussing these questions, hand out **Recipe for Peace in Your Dating Life** (pages 70-71) to each girl, and work through it as a group.

After you and your teens have talked through the handout, ask a few closing questions—

• *We've had some good discussion on the topics of dating and guys. What have you found to be most helpful? Least helpful?*
• *What actions do you want to be different because of this session?*
• *What might you need to help make those changes a reality?*

The information contained in **Recipe for Peace in Your Dating Life** is taken from *Sex & Dating: Let's Talk About It*, a video seminar by Mike and Eva Ashburn. Mike Ashburn also has presented this seminar to thousands of teens across the country. It's biblically sound, culturally relevant, and dignified. To order the video or to book a live appearance, contact Gospel Seed Productions, P.O. Box 546, Fishers, IN 46038, 800-341-9902.

When you've finished, close with something like this—

Your sexuality as a young woman is an indescribable and miraculous thing that is designed by God. Along with your mind, heart, and soul, it helps to define who you are. Because it is a gift from God, it should be treated as such—with respect, with obedience, with honor, and with selfish desires put aside.

> **quote**
>
> "I've learned that you can be in love with four girls at the same time."
>
> —age 9

Your body is a sacred creation of God's. Your heart is a sacred creation of God's. Don't let anyone use or abuse them.

> **quote**
>
> "I've learned that a teenager's biggest fear is the fear of a broken heart."
>
> —age 16

Give them a few minutes to share their answers with each other.

Close with a prayer that goes something like this—

Holy God, we are amazed at the miracle of the human body. And we are silenced by the awesome gift of sexuality. Help us to remember that many of the world's messages about sexuality are false. Our culture has taken something good and twisted it into something bad. God, if we have ever done that ourselves, please forgive us. As we mature into women of faith, we don't want to lose sight of your perfect plan for our lives. Amen.

─ closing ─

Takin' It to Heart

Have the girls break into pairs and answer the following questions—

> **You'll need—**
>
> • Copies of **On the Home Front** (page 72), one for each student

➤ What new ideas about dating and sexuality are you leaving with tonight?

➤ Should I hold you accountable for adhering to the dating guideline we talked about tonight? If not me, is there someone you'll ask this week to hold you accountable?

As students leave, distribute **On the Home Front** (page 72).

> How beautiful you are, my darling! Oh, how beautiful! Your eyes are doves.
>
> —Song of Songs 1:15

> All handouts are posted at
> www.YouthSpecialties.com/store/downloads
> password: women
> in plain text, Rich Text Format,
> MS Word 95/6.0, and PDF formats.
> Buyers of *Girls* can use them for *free!*

Whose dating line is it anyway?

Read the following situations one at a time. Give the sample answer if you like. Have several students select a prop and give an answer.

Worst ask-out line from a guy

So, do you want to go catch some WWF with me on Friday?

Worst guy conversation starter

Do you always paint your nails such a pukey color?

Worst girl conversation starter

Is that cologne you're wearing or did you spill in Chemistry?

Worst way for guy to ask out a cheerleader

I notice you like to yell a lot so do you want to go with me to a pig-calling contest?

Worst way for guy to ask out a serious student

I need a little help on my algebra. Wanna come over to my place?

Worst way for girl to ask out guy

My friend likes you, but she and I are really competitive so would you go out with me just to spite her?

Worst thing your dad could say to your date

Make sure to have her home exactly one-half hour from now.

Worst thing your date could say to your dad.

Don't worry. I haven't had any traffic violations yet this week.

Worst thing to say when your date gives you flowers

Red roses? You know I like yellow.

Check out these date traits, then buy $47 worth of the ones you most want in a guy you date. Place a check in the box beside your choices. Your total bill must be exactly $47 (not one dollar more or less). Happy shopping!

$10 Ten Dollar Traits

❑ smart
❑ Christian
❑ honest
❑ good sense of humor
❑ easy to talk to
❑ good looking
❑ student leader in his youth group
❑ ✻ your choice, not listed on this page _____

$5 Five Dollar Traits

❑ respects his parents
❑ nice to everyone at school
❑ volunteers at community charities
❑ has his own car
❑ starter on a varsity sport
❑ has a good-paying part-time job
❑ teaches Sunday School to younger kids

$1 One Dollar Traits

❑ holds doors open for women
❑ tall
❑ gets good grades
❑ Homecoming king
❑ goes to my church
❑ leads a Bible study at school

Not too easy, was it? Now pretend that money is no object. It doesn't matter what your bill totals. Pick your top 10 favorite traits by circling them

I Corinthians 6 (verses 12-15) *The Message*

Just because something is technically legal doesn't mean that it's spiritually appropriate. If I went around doing whatever I thought I could get by with, I'd be a slave to my whims.

You know the old saying, "First you eat to live, and then you live to eat"? Well, it may be true that the body is only a temporary thing, but that's no excuse for stuffing your body with food, or indulging it with sex. Since the Master honors you with a body, honor him with your body! Remember that your bodies are created with the same dignity as the Master's body.

I Thessalonians 4 (verses 1-3) *The Message*

One final word, friends. We ask you—*urge* is more like it—that you keep on doing what we told you to do to please God, not in a dogged religios plod, but in a living, spirited dance. You know the guidelines we laid out for you from the Master Jesus. God wants you to live a pure life.

Keep yourselves from sexual promiscuity.

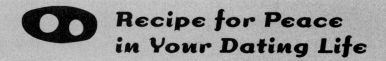

In General...

Girls are led by their emotions and their hearts. Guys are led by their eyes and their imaginations.

What implications does that have for you in dating? In school? In clothing choices? In physical movement?

According to some people, *Guys give love to get sex; Girls give sex to get love.*

In what ways do you see these statements as true? As false?

Let's say, for the sake of discussion, that the statements are true. How does that make the guy feel? The girl? Explain your answer.

For as high as the heavens are above the earth, so great is his love for those who fear him; as far as the east is from the west, so far has he removed our transgressions from us.
—*Psalm 103:12* NIV

If we confess our sins, he is faithful and just and will forgive us our sins and purify us from all unrighteousness.
—*1 John 1:9* NIV

Though your sins are like scarlet, they shall be as white as snow; though they are red as crimson, they shall be like wool.
—*Isaiah 1:18* NIV

If someone has had sexual intercourse before marriage and he or she asks God for forgiveness, God delivers on his promise. In God's eyes, that person is pure.

Do you believe the last statement is true? Why or why not?

If God now sees the person as pure, does that mean the person won't experience any effects from the sexual experience? Explain your answer.

The ideas in Recipe for Peace in Your Dating Life are adapted from the video *Dating and Sexuality: Let's Talk about It* by Mike and Eva Ashburn (Gospel Seed Productions, 1997). Used with permission. All rights reserved.

Think About It

The minute you start drawing lines on yourself and each other that mean, "Off limits on this side; good to go on this other side," you have reduced yourself to a sexual object.

What does this mean for a Christian teenager?

Don't play mind games with each other.

What do you think this statement means?

Guys should ask out girls face to face.

Do you agree with this statement? Why or why not?

When a guy asks out a girl, there are only two possible answers—yes or no.

But what if you don't want to hurt the guy's feelings? Shouldn't you let him down easy by giving him an excuse?

The Only Dating Guideline You'll Ever Need

Limit yourself to kissing, hugging, and holding hands...and that may be too much for some.

Why only kissing, hugging, and holding hands?
Because most of the trouble starts after that.

But when might kissing, hugging, and holding hands be too much?
When it makes a guy or girl want more than just that.

When it makes a guy or girl imagine impure thoughts.

(And if the previous two results are true for you, you should examine more closely your kissing, hugging, and holding hands.)

When you're thinking about kissing a guy you don't know very well, ask yourself these questions—
What's my reason for kissing him? (Think about what your kiss communicates to him.)

Am I treating him in a way that's consitent with biblical principles—to respect others and act in their best interests?

Think about the dating guideline—

Limit yourself to kissing, hugging, and holding hands…and that may be too much for some.

Journal about any thoughts or questions you might have.

MEMORY VERSE
Keep This in Mind

But among you there must not be even a hint of sexual immorality, or of any kind of impurity, or of greed, because these are improper for God's holy people.

—*Ephesians 5:3*

PRAYER
Put Your Hands Together

Dear Father, I have so many questions about my sexuality, about guys, and about the relationships that I have with guys. Things can be so confusing. And painful. And wonderful. And terrible. And great. And everything else. My greatest desire is that you would be in control of my entire life. It feels weird to say, "God, please teach me about dating and sexuality," but that's what I want—your guidance and truth. Amen.

THOUGHT
For Your Gray Matter

Your relationship with God must be the defining factor in all your other relationships.

Dear Parents,

On Wednesday evenings we're working through *Girls: 10 Gutsy, God-Centered Sessions on Issues That Matter to Girls* and *Guys: 10 Fearless, Faith-Focused Sessions on Issues That Matter to Guys*. The guys and girls are meeting in separate groups during this time so that they're better able to discuss issues that are relevant to them. While guys and girls are concerned with many of the same issues—friends, parents, future plans, emotions—this curriculum helps them approach the subjects from their unique viewpoints.

In a few weeks, we will be tackling the issue of dating and sexuality. Certainly the world's view of dating and sexuality is anything but God-centered, so it's a challenging topic. We want to reassure you that, though we will be encouraging very open and honest discussion and though we will welcome any questions your daughter or son may have, we are committed to—

- presenting biblical truths
- steering students toward a godly view of dating
- honoring your sacred role as parents

If you have any questions or if you would like to see the lessons we'll be using, please call me at the church office.

Thank you for the privilege of being a small part of your child's journey toward a deeper and more mature faith.

In His Grip,

Hershel Berzacky
Youth Director

⬤ THE ISSUE

True love waits. It's all over the teenage Christian media. It's the only way to be pure in God's sight. But Jesus was just as interested in following the spirit of the law as he was in following the letter of the law, which means minds must be as pure as bodies. Therein lies the challenge.

introduction
Delvin' In

In our culture of glorified sexuality, it's a big challenge for anyone—but especially teens, who are becoming sexually mature—to commit to and follow through on a goal of living a physically pure life. Guys are encouraged to demonstrate their manhood by having sex with the hottest girls they can entice. Girls are encouraged to demonstrate their sexiness—what the world considers to be the highlight of femininity—by dressing, walking, and acting in a way that catches the eyes and stirs the hormones of whichever guys might be watching. Even if your Christian students have rejected the world's messages about physical purity, it's hard to ignore the signs.

Perhaps the greatest challenge for teenage believers is not protecting their bodies' purity but rather their hearts' purity. Girls who choose to save sexual intercourse for marriage are nonetheless exposed to extramarital sex in even

quote

"Our youth culture teaches preteens to dress to be sexy. Before their breasts are much more than buds, they are learning how to dress provocatively. But of course it's not called provocative. Rather the style is sold as Fun! In style! Cute! All the rage!"

—Lisa Graham McMinn in Growing Strong Daughters
(Baker Books, 2000, page 157)

the mildest of movies and are bombarded with tales of romantic love, which, for a woman, is Step One toward sexual fulfillment. Girls who choose to save sexual intercourse for marriage may unwillingly find themselves thinking about it, fantasizing about it, and dreaming of one day experiencing it with their own Prince Charming.

Many girls who have chosen to save sexual intercourse for marriage are filling that physical void with chick flicks, romance novels, soap operas, and prime time dramas. Why? Because seeing and reading about it stirs a girl's emotions, and a girl's emotions are closely linked to her sexuality.

> But don't think you've preserved your virtue simply by staying out of bed. Your *heart* can be corrupted by lust even quicker than you *body*. Those leering looks you think nobody notices—they also corrupt.
>
> —*Jesus from Matthew 5*, The Message

It's *natural* to think about sex. It's *okay* to think about sex. If more people thought about sex rationally there might not be so much irrational behavior. But it is *not okay* to imagine oneself having sexual intercourse outside of marriage.

Jesus challenges us to follow the spirit of the law, not just the letter of the law. The letter of the law says, "Don't engage in sex before marriage." The spirit of the law says, "Don't *imagine* engaging in sex before marriage."

Retaining one's physical purity is a challenge. Retaining one's emotional and mental purity is more like waging a war. It's much, much harder! Help your students devise spiritual and practical ways to accomplish this.

Warmin' Up

And the Winner Is . . .

Divide your students into groups of three or four. Hand out pens and copies of **And the Winner Is...** (page 80) to each group. This is a small-scale People's Choice Awards activity. Tell the girls they must come to an agreement on every answer. Give them seven to 10 minutes to finish.

> **You'll need—**
> • Copies of **And the Winner Is...** (page 80), one for each group
> • Pens

Then gather everyone together and ask the following questions—

> ➤ What do your group's favorite movies have in common?
> ➤ What three things do you think have to be in a movie in order for a girl to like it?
> ➤ What do your group's favorite TV shows have in common?
> ➤ What three things do you think have to be in a TV show for a girl to get hooked on it?
> ➤ How do you feel when you watch a couple fall in love on the screen or read about it in a book?

Diggin' a Little Deeper

Say something like this as you move into the next section—

> *Most women enjoy watching and reading love stories. The story becomes real to them. They almost experience it for themselves. It doesn't seem like there'd be anything wrong with that. But a woman's emotions influence her thoughts. If watching or reading about something leads her thoughts down the wrong path, then something should be done about it.*

Choose one or more of the following activities—

option [group video activity]
Where Have All the Movies Gone?

One of goals for this session is to help students recognize that what they watch and see can have a measurable effect on their thoughts and actions. It's next to impossible to find current movies containing scenes that promote—or demonstrate—physical and personal purity. (If one ever appears on the video store shelves, by all means use it!) And this topic doesn't lend itself to learning-the-good-by-observing-the-bad. So you'll have to pursue this discussion without a corresponding video clip.

You might want to introduce these questions with something like this—

> Get out while you can; get out of this sick and stupid culture!
> —*from Acts 2*, The Message

> *I wanted to show you a video clip that showed a romantic couple making good decisions about their purity— both in their actions, their thoughts, and their words. But I couldn't find one.*

> ➤ Can you think of any current, popular movies where the characters make a conscious decision to refrain from sex outside of marriage, to avoid tempting situations, or to behave, dress, or speak in a way that discourages sexual topics rather than encourages them?
> ➤ Do you think producers of movies—and other media—make a conscious attempt to promote sexual immorality? If so, what do you think the reason might be?
> ➤ When you watch a movie that has sexual content—even a brief scene—that doesn't fit into God's design (sex before marriage, adultery), do you consider that movie to be impure? Explain your reasoning.

> Why is it okay—or not okay—to expose yourself to movies, videos, TV, et cetera, that contain impure sexual content?

> What might God say if you asked him whether it's okay for you to watch, see, read, or listen to something that has a little bit of impure content? A lot of impure content? Explain where your ideas come from if you can.

> How would you define impurity when it comes to the things you see, read, watch, and listen to?

option [individual video activity]
What You See Is What You Are

Many popular movies have one or more romantic scenes. If you have a few videos on your shelf you won't even have to rent one for this activity. Pass out

You'll need—
- A video clip of a romantic scene
- TV and VCR
- Copies of **What You See Is What You Are** (page 81), one for each student
- Pens

What You See Is What You Are (page 81) before showing the video clip and point out that the girls should be aware of their feelings as they watch. Show the clip and ask your students the following questions—

> Do you think the romantic tales that are told in books, in movies, or on TV have affected your view of what it will be like when you fall in love with someone? In what way?

> What expectations about romantic love do you think you've acquired from books, movies, videos, and television shows? How realistic do you think those expectations are? (Note to married youth workers: Do not, do not, do not laugh at their answers. Someday they'll discover the truth all on their own.)

You're blessed when you get your inside world—your mind and heart—put right. Then you can see God in the outside world.
—*Jesus from Matthew 5, The Message*

After showing the video clip, have the girls fill out **What You See Is What You Are.** Their answers will remain completely private. Reassure them that no one else, not even you, will see them. They will throw them away as soon as the activity is over. Encourage them to be very honest with themselves.

After they've had some time to do this, ask some follow-up questions—

> How does what you see affect your emotions?

> How do your emotions affect your thoughts?

> Do you ever imagine what it would be like for you to be in the situation that you're watching or reading about? If yes, why do you suppose you do that?

> If you find yourself thinking impure thoughts—about sexual activity, for example—what can you do to stop those thoughts?

> What can you do to prevent those thoughts in the first place? (Let this discussion question go as long as necessary. It hits at the very heart of the matter.)

Give your teens an opportunity to tear up their worksheets and throw them away.

option [individual silent activity]
Blessed Are the Pure in Heart

Hand out a copy of **Blessed Are the Pure in Heart** (page 82) to each girl. Say something like—

You'll need—
- Copies of **Blessed Are the Pure in Heart** (page 82), one for each girl
- CD player
- Worship CD

The Bible has a lot to say about the importance of purity. The majority of what it has to say is not about the purity of one's actions but the purity of one's heart. You're going to have the opportunity to read God's words about purity and meditate on them.

Nudgers (nuj´erz) *n.* a tool used to gently push teens toward new insight

➤ Imagine being in love and engaged for seven years.
➤ Imagine the joy of being sexually pure at your wedding—a joy that makes all the waiting seem "like only a few days" because of your love for your fiancé.

When you're ready for your students to begin, play worship music softly. There are no questions on the worksheet, just Scripture. Give your girls enough time to close their eyes and really soak up God's Word. Regroup for some discussion—

quote

"Anything that is good, praiseworthy, true, honorable, right, pure, beautiful, and respected—that is what should fill your mind. How much of what you read—and listen to and think about—during a day passes those tests?"

—Kevin Johnson in What Do Ya Know? *(Bethany House, 2000)*

➤ How often do you specifically ask God to examine your heart?
➤ How would you feel about letting another person examine your heart—your inner thoughts and feelings—throughout the day?
➤ In what ways can you begin to examine your own heart more honestly?
➤ What most prevents you from having a pure heart?

Bible study

Gettin' into the Word

Jacob Marries Leah and Rachel
Genesis 29:14-30

Have you ever noticed that there aren't many uplifting marriage stories in the Bible? There's more mention of adultery, incest, enticement, harems, and husbands who were "forced" to sleep with the maidservant than there is of communication, compromise, and courting. The story of Jacob, Leah, and Rachel

You'll need—
• Bibles

certainly doesn't have much to offer for Happy and Healthy Marriage Guidelines, but it does offer a glimpse of young love and courtship lived out with honor and integrity. That should be the focus of your discussion.

Move into the Bible study with a few comments like—

There's no question about it—God wants us to have a pure heart. It's not his way of controlling us or making our lives miserable. Rather it's his way of freeing us—from the harmful effects of frustrated and sinful thoughts—and of making our lives joy-filled—by giving us the opportunity to focus our minds on things that are within God's design, such as beauty, kindness, holiness, love, hope, and joy.

Have a few volunteers take turns reading through Genesis 29:14-30. When the reading is done, remind your students that Old Testament marriage customs were very different from those of today. Tell them you're going to focus on the courtship, the commitment, and the sexual purity in the story.

Discuss the following—

➤ For seven years, Jacob worked for and lived with Rachel's family. Describe the challenges of that situation for an unmarried couple.
➤ What are some of the strategies that Jacob and Rachel might have used in staying sexually pure for seven years?
➤ What challenges do you face in today's world that Jacob and Rachel did not have to face back then?

➤ Do you think it's possible to keep your mind sexually pure in today's world? Explain.

— closing —
Takin' It to Heart

End the session with something like this—

You'll need—
• **CD and CD Player**
• Copies of **On the Home Front** (page 83), one for each student.

In most ways, it's easier to commit oneself to physical purity than to heart purity.

Physical purity is easily measured. Heart purity is not.

> Summing it all up, friends, I'd say you'll do best by filling your minds and meditating on things true, noble, reputable, authentic, compelling, gracious—the best, not the worst; the beautiful, not the ugly; things to praise, not things to curse.
> —from Philippians 4, The Message

Physical purity is hard to ignore. Heart purity is easy to ignore.

Physical purity—or lack of it—can be difficult to hide. Heart purity is easily hidden—except from God.

God loves you no matter what you choose to do, but because he loves so much, he wants what's best for you. He might be trying to get your attention this very night.

After sharing your closing thoughts with your students, play some soft music as the backdrop to a time of contemplation and prayer. Ask the girls to close their eyes and then guide them in prayerful contemplation with these thoughts—

quote

"Gals: When you choose swimwear spun from a single spool of dental floss you might as well mail the guys invitations to your birthday suit."
—*Kevin Johnson in* What Do Ya Know? *(Bethany House, 2000)*

➤ Ask God to show you the parts of your life that might be impure.
➤ Ask God to show you the parts of your life that might be physically or emotionally unhealthy.
➤ Ask God to show you how you can change or get rid of those parts of your life.

Make a comment like this to introduce the prayer—

Those who want to pledge to live a life of heart purity can pray with me, silently affirming the words in your heart. Those who aren't ready to make that pledge can choose to simply listen to the prayer.

Pray with words like these—

God, on this night, we want to give our hearts to you fully. We aren't just committing our actions to you. We aren't just paying you lip service. We aren't just saying words because we think we should. We truly want to have clean and pure hearts.

We can't do it ourselves. We are so weak when it comes to our hearts and minds. We need your strength and guidance, God. Only you can give us the desire for a pure heart, and only you can give us the grace to pursue it. That's what we want.

We want to know you more fully. We want to love you more deeply. We want to honor you with pure hearts. Amen.

Hand out **On the Home Front** (page 83) as students leave.

All handouts are posted at
www.YouthSpecialties.com/store/downloads
password: women
in plain text, Rich Text Format,
MS Word 95/6.0, and PDF formats.
Buyers of *Girls* can use them for *free!*

And the Winner Is...

As a group, come up with your top selections for the following categories. You must all agree on the choices.

Favorite Movies

1.
2.
3.
4.
5.

Favorite Television Show

1.
2.
3.
4.
5.

Favorite Male Celebrity

1.
2.
3.
4.
5.

What qualities do you want in movies that you like to watch over and over again? Make a list.

What You See Is What You Are

As you watch the video clip, think about the emotions stirred in you. Then take a look at what thoughts those emotions bring to your mind. Write them below.

No one except you will read this. Be honest. God already knows your secret thoughts, so you won't surprise him.

Blessed Are the Pure in Heart

While you listen to the worship music, read through these verses. Think about them. Don't rush. Don't feel pressured. It takes some time to quiet yourself. Close your eyes. Meditate on—fill your mind with—God's words. Think about what God might be communicating to you. If you listen, he promises to respond.

May the words of my mouth and the meditation of my heart be pleasing in your sight, O Lord, my Rock and my Redeemer.

—*Psalm 19:14*

Who may ascend the hill of the Lord? Who may stand in his holy place? He who has clean hands and a pure heart.

—*Psalm 24:3-4*

Test me, O Lord, and try me, examine my heart and my mind; for your love is ever before me, and I walk continually in your truth.

—*Psalms 26:2-3*

Create in me a pure heart, O God, and renew a steadfast spirit within me.

—*Psalm 51:10*

Search me, O God, and know my heart; test me and know my anxious thoughts.

—*Psalm 139:23*

Finally, [sisters], whatever is true, whatever is noble, whatever is right, whatever is pure, whatever is lovely, whatever is admirable—if anything is excellent or praiseworthy—think about such things.

—*Philippians 4:8*

Above all else, guard your heart, for it is the wellspring of life.

—*Proverbs 4:23*

Read Philippians 4:8 (below) several times this week. Then think or journal about this—

Having inner purity may require giving up something you're hanging on to. What is it? Are you ready for that? If not, what can you do to change that?

— MEMORY VERSE —
Keep This in Mind

Finally, brothers, whatever is true, whatever is noble, whatever is right, whatever is pure, whatever is lovely, whatever is admirable—if anything is excellent or praiseworthy—think about such things.
—*Philippians 4:8*

— PRAYER —
Put Your Hands Together

Dear God,
Protecting my mind from impure thoughts isn't easy. Give me wisdom as I choose what to watch, what to read, what to listen to, and who to be around. If I need to give up something, help me do that. Help me find alternatives that will honor you. Amen.

— THOUGHT —
For Your Gray Matter

Pure is not simply an adjective; it's a way of life.

Friends Forever
Or, you mean I can't have my friends over?!

⊙ THE ISSUE

A teenage girl's relationship with her friends runs strong and deep. So what does Jesus have to say about being a friend?

---

introduction
Delvin' In

There is nothing quite as special as having a best friend. Girls are pros at making and being a best friend. You see them all over—at the mall, in your youth group, at school, catching a movie, munching on burgers and fries...best friends are, like, totally awesome.

But you've probably also seen the lone girl who doesn't hang at the mall with anyone, sits on the fringes at youth group, eats alone in the school cafeteria, watches only rental movies because she has no one to go to the theater with. Not having a best friend—or not having *any* friend at all—is a great tragedy in a teenage girl's life.

During the high school years, friends have more influence than parents. Friends know secrets that parents don't. Friends will stay up all night talking. If a girl could choose who to spend her weekend with, it would probably be her

quote

> "Friendship is more delicate than love."
> —Hester Lynch Piozz

friends, not her mom, dad, and little brother. Most women have a deep sense of loyalty to their friends. They're usually emotionally attached. They experience bonding known as kindred spirithood.

It's an amazing thing.

But being a good friend doesn't always come naturally. Extending friendships beyond a circle of one or two can sometimes lead to all kinds of

messy situations: who gets to sit next to whom at lunch, who will be the decision maker and ruling queen, who will feel left out of the sacred inner circle, who will be the favorite of all, who will be on top of the ladder, who will be at the bottom...

Friendship is one of God's great gifts to humankind. When he created Eve, it was because

> I have a serious concern to bring up with you, my friends, using the authority of Jesus, our Master. I'll put it as urgently as I can; You *must* get along with each other. You must learn to be considerate of one another, cultivating a life in common.
> —from I Corinthians I, The Message

Adam needed a companion and mate. Long before a girl needs a mate, she needs companions. Just as it was with Adam, it's not good for her to be alone.

Enter: friends.

Best friends, social friends, so-so friends, fair-weather friends, temporary friends, lifelong friends—you name it, it's out there. Since friends occupy perhaps the largest part of a young woman's heart—taking second place to God if the young woman is a Christian— then certainly it's worth spending some time focusing on these important relationships.

And even though your students may think they know everything about friendship, it's worth giving them the opportunity to learn just a little bit more.

Warmin' Up

The Friendship Gamble

When your girls arrive, give them a quick lesson in poker hands—

actually these are modified poker hands. (No, they're not going to play poker. You're using Uno cards.) These are the sets they need to know—

> - pair (two of the same number, any color)
> - three of a kind (three of the same number, any color)
> - run (three cards in sequential order, any color)
> - flush (five cards of the same color, any numbers)
> - straight flush (five cards of the same color, in sequential order)
> - full house (one pair plus three of a kind)

quote

"The best times in life are made a thousand times better when shared with a dear friend."
—*Luci Swindoll in* You Bring the Confetti...God Brings the Joy *(Word, 1997)*

Hand out between two and five cards to each girl—five if your group is small, fewer if your group is large. If your group is on the smaller side, be sure you can make several combinations of each set with the cards you give out. Explain to the girls that when you call a set, such as three of a kind or full house, they must group up with other girls to create it. Even if a student has all the necessary cards by herself, she *must* group up with at least one other person. Scuffling around, yelling, trying to manipulate the person who's holding a red three to join this group instead of that—can you think of any greater way to spend your time?

The first group to form the correct hand wins. Call out the next hand. Play about 10 rounds (more or less as your time allows).

When you've finished, collect the cards and talk about the activity—

> - How did you figure out who you needed to group up with?
> - If there were two different people whose cards would have given you the winning hand, how did you decide between the two?
> - In real life, how do you decide who you want to group up with or be friends with?
> - If you're friends with several different groups of girls, how do you decide who you'll spend time with?

Diggin' a Little Deeper

Move into the next activity with something like this—

Your friends are probably some of the most important people in your life. Friendships help make you who you are, have a part in defining your personality, and often affect the choices you make. Today we're going to look at friendship more closely and hopefully learn something about God's plan for those relationships.

Choose one or more of the following options.

option [group activity]
Setting Your Friendship Criteria

Before you begin, label the five containers with the following headings: HONESTY, SENSE OF HUMOR, SIMILAR INTERESTS, FAITH and CREATIVITY. Across the top of the whiteboard, make headings with the same labels.

Give each of your girls 15 voting tokens. Explain to them that you're going to conduct an anonymous vote regarding friends. In African tribes, it used to be a custom to vote on issues until the result was unanimous, even if that meant voting more than once. They voted by dropping small stones into a bowl. Today, your girls are going to do something similar, though they don't have to have unanimous decisions.

> A friend is always loyal.
>
> —*Proverb 17:17,* NLT

Explain it to your girls this way—

Each of you has 15 voting tokens. If you look around the room, you'll see 5 voting containers. Each one is labeled with a specific characteristic that a friend might have. With your 15 tokens, you must vote on the importance of each characteristic to you. You must put 5 tokens in one container, 4, 3, 2, and 1 in the remaining containers. We'll count the tokens to see which characteristic was voted most important, and we'll look at the order of the other four choices. This is an anonymous vote. No discussion. No peeking. If someone is voting, stay back until they're done.

quote

"To have a good friend is one of the highest delights of life; to be a good friend is one of the noblest and most difficult undertakings."

—*from* God's Little Instruction Book on Friendship
(Honor Books, 1996, page 10)

Depending on the number of girls you have, this will probably take between one and five minutes. You might want to play some music—*upbeat* music, mind you—during the activity.

When the voting is completed, choose five girls who will each count the votes in one bucket. Record the final tallies on the whiteboard for everyone to see.

Then ask these questions—

> - How did you choose which characteristic was most important to you? Least important?
> - In choosing friends, do you consider the ranking order you just voted on? For example, if you think honesty is the most important characteristic and sense of humor is the least, would you choose not to be friends with someone who is very funny but only sometimes honest? Explain.
> - If your most important criterion for a friend isn't on this list, what is it?
> - Do you think it's okay to have "friend criteria"? Or should you make friends without considering these or other characteristics? Explain.

option [video activity]
Now and Then

Four girls are spending a summer day together, displaying many different facets of girl friendships. Show the clip.

You'll need—

- *Now and Then*
- TV and VCR

0:31:43 The girls are riding bikes while "Knock Three Times" plays on the radio.
0:35:22 Roberta says, "It was a joke."

Ask questions like—

> - How do girls create—or become—a group of friends?
> - Within a group of several friends, do all the girls play equal roles? Are all of

> Laugh with your happy friends when they're happy; share tears when they're down. Get along with each other; don't be stuck-up. Make friends with nobodies; don't be the great somebody.
>
> —*from Romans 12,* The Message

them treated equally? Why do you think that?

➤ Why do girls react so strongly to what their friends say and do?

➤ Think about your group of friends. When you have a free day to spend together, what do you like to do? How might you like to change that (stop gossiping, helping at the library together, praying together, getting more exercise)?

option [individual activity]
Kindred Spirits

Give a pen and a copy of **Kindred Spirits** (page 91) to each girl. Tell them you're going to let

You'll need—
• Copies of **Kindred Spirits** (page 91), one for each girl
• Pens

them walk down memory lane and think about the different best friends they've had. After giving them several minutes to work through the handout, ask some questions—

➤ What similarities did you find in the descriptions of your best friends?

➤ What changes do you see in your friendships as you've grown older?

➤ What were the reasons for changing from one best friend to another?

➤ What are the advantages of having a single best friend? The disadvantages?

➤ If you've ever ended a friendship, what caused it? How did you end it? Would you handle it differently now?

option [another individual activity]
Buy a Friend

Give your students a few minutes to fill out **Buy a Friend** (page 92), a shopping profile for a

You'll need—
• Copies of **Buy a Friend** (page 92), one for each girl
• Pens

friend. Then ask about their thoughts with questions like these—

➤ In real life, have you ever found yourself wishing one of your friends was just a little bit different? Why is that?

➤ Have you ever had a friend make unrealistic demands on you, such as having to spend all your time together or not allowing you to be friends with anyone she doesn't like? How did you deal with this?

➤ How is your relationship with Jesus like your earthly friendships? How is it different?

➤ Do you think it's possible to know God—an invisible spirit—as well as you know your friends? Explain.

Bible study

Gettin' into the Word

Friends in the Bible
Selected verses

After finishing, move into the Bible study with something like this—

You'll need—
• Bibles

> *God is the creator of friendship. It says in the Bible that all good things come from him, and true friendship is a good thing—though we've all probably experienced so-called friendships that aren't so good, too.*
>
> *We're going to look at some verses in the Bible that talk about friends. Then as a group, we'll try to figure out what that means for each of us.*

Ask a volunteer to read a passage. Then discuss it with the questions provided or others of your own. You can use any or all of the verses here.

Psalm 41:9

This is a psalm of David at a time when he was very ill. Because of his sickness and possible upcoming death, his enemies were watching closely to see what would happen. To David, it felt like his enemies were after him. For some reason, he also concluded that his best friend—a person he trusted, loved, and confided in—was no longer looking after his—David's—interests. Make sure your girls take note of David's very honest emotions.

➤ How did David deal with his strong emotions?
➤ What might cause someone to be rejected or abandoned by a friend?
➤ How might each person feel? Be specific and explain your thoughts.
➤ How have you dealt with a similar situation?

John 11:5 and John 10:38-39

When we think of Jesus' friends, we usually think of the 12 disciples first. But Jesus didn't just have male friends. There were many women who were part of the group that followed him. Mary and Martha were clearly friends of Jesus. He often went to their home, shared meals, had conversations, and hung out around the table enjoying the company.

The question of whether girls can have guy friends without being romantically involved is often asked. If Jesus is our example, then the answer seems clear—yes they can.

In fact, some people prefer guy-girl friendships. Many girls like to have guy friends because there isn't gossip, catty backbiting, and other negative aspects often present in some girl-girl friendships. And guys often like to have girl friends because they have a hard time talking to other guys about things that are important to them.

➤ What's your view of guy-girl friendships? Talk about that.
➤ What are some of the advantages of guy-girl friendships? Some of the disadvantages?
➤ What are some of the dangers of guy-girl friendships?

Proverbs 22:24-25

God's word is very clear on one thing—a Christian's total responsibility is to love God and love others. As Jesus said, all the laws and all the prophets can be summed up in those two commandments. So if we're supposed to *love* everyone, does that mean we're supposed to *be friends* with everyone?

From these two verses, it doesn't seem like it. *Loving* is often about displaying actions that reflect godliness to another person. *Friendship*, at least for teenagers, is more about sharing common interests, spending time together, having a person to call on no matter what, no matter when.

➤ Is "loving others" the same as "liking others?" Talk through your ideas.
➤ If God doesn't expect us to be friends with everyone (as Proverbs 22 seems to indicate), what does he expect from us?
➤ What are some ways that you can love people who aren't your friends?
➤ Name traits or behaviors you want to avoid when choosing friends. Explain why.
➤ Jesus was a friend *to* everyone. Is that different than being friends *with* everyone? Explain.

Close the session with something like this—

There aren't many examples of female friends in the Bible, but that's probably because the Bible was written during a time when women's lives weren't discussed very much. You can bet that there were as many best friends back then as there are now. Making friends comes easily to some people. For others it's more difficult.

One thing is clear—God wants you to be friendly to everyone you meet.

God wants you to have some good friends in your life. And God knows it's important for you to have friends who will influence you to do good. The friends you have now will have a part in shaping who you are—and you can have a part in shaping them!

closing

Takin' It to Heart

As you close, have all the girls join in a large circle so they can pledge their friendship to each other. This is a great chance for them to make a visible pact with one another.

You'll need—

- **Ink pad**
- **CD and CD player**
- **Copies of On the Home Front** (page 93), **one for each student**

Pick a girl to start the cycle (or you can start it yourself if you'd like to be included). Have her

press one thumb on the ink pad, then press it against the next girl's thumb. This can be done without speaking while soft music plays in the background, or the girls can say something like, "I pledge to be your friend as a fellow human being and as a daughter of God."

Then the second girls presses her other thumb on the ink pad, presses it against the next girl's thumb, and continues the cycle. When the ink pad gets to the last girl, she'll press her thumb against the first girl's inkless thumb, and the friendship circle will be complete.

As your girls leave, hand out **On the Home Front** (page 93).

quote

"Anybody can sympathize with the sufferings of a friend, but it requires a very fine nature to sympathize with a friend's success."

—*Oscar Wilde*

All handouts are posted at
www.YouthSpecialties.com/store/downloads
password: women
in plain text, Rich Text Format,
MS Word 95/6.0, and PDF formats.
Buyers of *Girls* can use them for *free!*

On the timeline below list all the best friends you've had whether it's one or 15. Write their names, the time in your life when you were friends with them, one event you shared with that friend that stands out in your mind, and three things that you liked about that person.

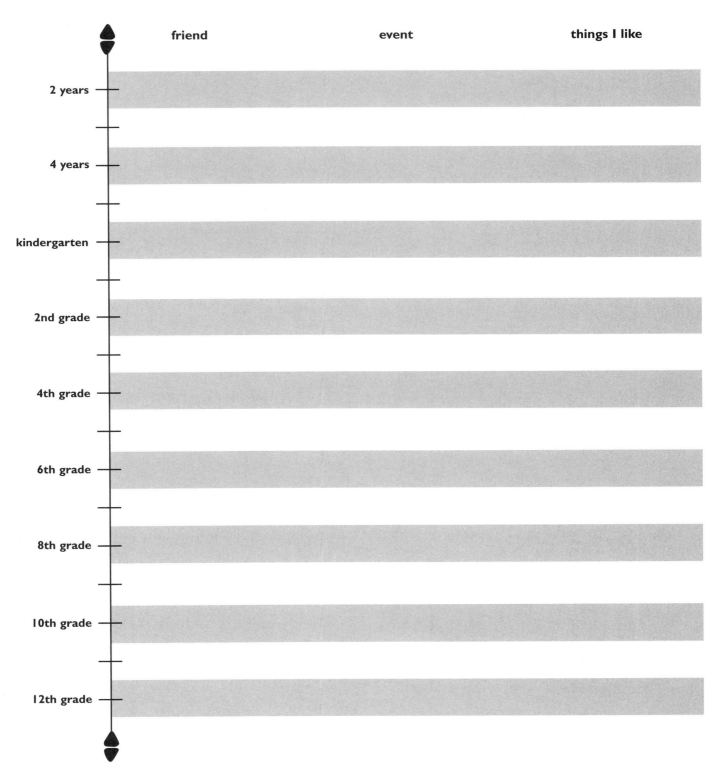

friend   event   things I like

2 years

4 years

kindergarten

2nd grade

4th grade

6th grade

8th grade

10th grade

12th grade

BUY A FRIEND $

You may spend exactly $25 on a friend. No more, no less. Put a check by the items you want to buy.

$2 EACH

- ☐ good-looking
- ☐ athletic
- ☐ smart
- ☐ cool clothes
- ☐ musical

$3 EACH

- ☐ talented
- ☐ honest
- ☐ has fun parents
- ☐ doesn't gossip
- ☐ loyal

$5 EACH

- ☐ accepts me as I am
- ☐ popular
- ☐ funny
- ☐ kind
- ☐ same interests as me

On the Home Front

This week read through the book of Proverbs, taking special note of the verses dealing with friendship. Journal or think about these questions—

What kind of friend are you to others?

Why is friendship such an important part of life?

┌─ MEMORY VERSE ─┐
Keep This in Mind

A friend loves at all times.
—*Proverbs 17:17*

┌─ PRAYER ─┐
Put Your Hands Together

God, thanks for the gift of friendship. Thanks for my closest friends. Help me to be a good friend to others. If there's someone at school you want me to befriend, show her to me. Amen.

┌─ THOUGHT ─┐
For Your Gray Matter

Friendships aren't *born*; they're *cultivated*.

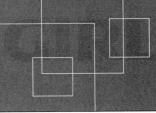
⊙ THE ISSUE

Up and down, round and round, in and out, over here and over there—that's often an accurate description of the dizzying path a young woman's emotions take. God created women, God created emotions, and by jove, e'er the twain shall meet.

---

introduction
Delvin' In

In case you haven't noticed, (most) women cry more than (most) men. For tangible evidence, just watch a male and female, side by side, watching Kodak commercials, the Special Olympics, and a slow motion, music-enhanced tribute to an overlooked hero.

Tears on one side.

"Are you *crying*?!" on the other side.

The fact that females tend to be more outwardly emotional than males is only compounded during the teen years thanks to all the changes that are taking place physically, sexually, emotionally, and brain-chemically.

For every young woman who sails through her teen years without a care in the world, there are hundreds more who are stuck on a roller coaster ride of joy, anger, sorrow, excitement, fear, trepidation, anguish, jealousy, loneliness, self-loathing, happiness…

For young women, it can be frightening to feel out of control of one's emotions. Some have described it as an out of body experience, like sitting across the room and observing one's self fall apart over a minor disappointment. Said one teen girl, "Sometimes I just want to shake her—me—really hard and say, 'Snap out of it!' but I know it won't do any good."

It may not be possible for a young woman—or anyone, for that matter—to simply pull herself up by her bootstraps and declare herself to be free from the power of her emotions. Nor will the honesty of, "Hello, my name is Sally, and I'm an emotional basket case," do much to help control the wild ride.

But if God created women, and if God created emotions, and if God introduced the two, then certainly he must have a plan for their peaceful coexistence. The young women in your group need to know about that plan.

---

opening activity
Warmin' Up

I Feel . . .

Before you begin, write each of the following words on a separate index card—

You'll need—
- 10 index cards
- Marker

ANGRY	AFRAID
HAPPY	EXCITED
SURPRISED	SAD
CONFUSED	STRESSED
STUNNED	JEALOUS

Ask for a volunteer. Explain that you'll give her a card that contains an emotion.

---

quote

"The feeling is a physical reaction; the emotion takes the feeling to the mental level, involving mind as well as body. It is not the initial feeling which causes us trouble, but the emotion which grows out of it."
—*Vincent P. Collins in* Me, Myself and You *(Abbey Press, 1974, page 43)*

She should express that emotion through facial expressions and body language (without using any words) while the rest of the group tries to figure out what the emotion is. Give her the card. When the group has guessed the emotion, repeat the process with a new volunteer and a new card.

When you've finished all the cards or you don't have any more volunteers, vote on the best "emoter." Discuss the activity—

- ➤ How do you know what most people are feeling—besides what they say?
- ➤ How can you read other people's faces accurately and know how they feel?
- ➤ What emotions are hardest to read? Easiest?

quote

"Feelings aren't facts! Just because you feel that a thing is so doesn't necessarily make it so."

—*Vincent P. Collins in* Me, Myself and You
(Abbey Press, 1974, page 48)

Say something like—

> ***God created us with the ability to experience emotions. However, he did not create us to be emotion-controlled creatures. Many females have strong emotional reactions to circumstances, what they hear, what they see, the way they're treated. It's no fun going through life feeling like you're on an out-of-control, emotional roller coaster. There must be a better way.***

quote

"While the *real you* can never completely overcome the influence of the *emotional you,* you must never let the *emotional you* get in the driver's seat. If you allow your feelings to dictate your behavior, you have become a driverless automobile, careening down the highway of life, headed for a crackup."

—*Vincent P. Collins in* Me, Myself and You *(Abbey Press, 1974, page 28)*

— exploring the topic —

Diggin' a Little Deeper

Choose one or more of the following activities.

option [group activity]
Name That Feeling

Divide your girls into groups of four or five. Give each group a copy of **Name That Feeling** (page 100)

You'll need—
- Copies of **Name That Feeling** (page 100), one for each group
- Pens

and a pen. Their job is to describe what they feel in response to each of the items. For example, beside, "When someone gossips about me, I feel…," they might write *angry.* Then they give a specific behavior that might result from that feeling, such as, "I say something mean about her, too," or "I feel like screaming at her."

When they've finished working on this handout, ask for volunteers to share some of their answers. Use questions like these for discussion—

- ➤ In your experience, do females—in general—tend to be extremely emotional? Talk about that.
- ➤ What are some of the dangers of emotions?
- ➤ What are some of the benefits of emotions?
- ➤ Tell about a time when you experienced strong—positive or negative—emotions. How did you act?
- ➤ How can a person who experiences strong emotions make rational and wise decisions?

option [video activity]
An Affair to Remember

option [individual activity]
I Feel, Therefore I Am

Show the clip from *Sleepless in Seattle* in which Suzy (Rita Wilson) is talking about the Cary Grant movie, "An Affair to Remember." She's sitting with her husband, Greg (Victor Garber), and brother Sam (Tom Hanks), who look at her like she's from another planet as she weeps and laughs and waves her hands around.

You'll need—
• *Sleepless in Seattle*
• TV and VCR

1:14:26 "You saw her in the airport?"
1:18:03 "I loved that movie."

Ask your students the following questions—

➤ Do women really get this emotional over things like a movie? Talk about that.
➤ Have you ever gotten emotionally involved in a movie, book or TV show? Describe your experience.
➤ Have you ever found yourself watching a certain movie over and over or reading a certain book over and over just to experience the emotions again? Explain.
➤ How do the guys you know—peers, relatives, other adults—view a woman's emotions?
➤ In your experience, are "female emotions" confusing to men? Explain.

Give each girl a copy of **I Feel, Therefore I Am** (page 101) and a pen. Explain that emotions often affect our behavior, some-

You'll need—
• Copies of **I Feel, Therefore I Am** (page 101), one for each girl
• Pens

times with negative results. The challenge for teen girls is not to stop feeling, but rather to *not let feelings dictate life*. In this activity, they'll compare times in their lives when they reacted because of their emotions rather than made choices based on facts or truth.

After they've had enough time to finish, gather as a group and ask for volunteers to share their responses. Then discuss some of the following—

➤ Which of the following statements do you think is more accurate? Talk about that.
  —Your emotions are an accurate reflection of reality.
  —Your emotions are a reflection of your own viewpoint.
➤ When you feel overwhelmed by your emotions, what do you do—or what can you do—to stay in control?
➤ What's your impression of people who are extremely emotional? Who act on their emotions only? Who seem to usually be one step away from crying or blowing up?
  ➤ In what ways can God help you control your emotions? Explain with specifics. (For example, he can help me act loving toward that person who always ticks me off no matter what she does.)

When Jesus saw her weeping, and the Jews who had come along with her also weeping, he was deeply moved in spirit and troubled. "Where have you laid him?" he asked. "Come and see, Lord," they replied. Jesus wept.

—John 11:33-35

Filled with compassion, Jesus reached out his hand and touched the man.

—Mark 1:41

Gettin' into the Word

Sarah and Hagar
Genesis 16, 21:1-21

After you've finished the previous activity, move into the Bible study with something like this—

You'll need—
- Copies of **The Story of Sarah and Hagar** (page 102), one for each girl
- Bibles
- Pens

 Nudgers (nuj´erz) *n.* a tool used to gently push teens toward new insight

- Sarah was afraid of being childless.
- Sarah was mad at—or at least frustrated with—God for allowing her to be barren.
- Sarah's response to these emotions was to compel her husband to have sex with her maidservant.
- When things turned sour between Sarah and her maidservant, she became angry with her husband.
- When Sarah's husband ignored her anger, she abused her maidservant.
- Her maidservant gave birth to Ishmael, who is believed to be the father of all Arabs.
- Sarah gave birth to a son, Isaac, and the Jewish nation.
- Think about the relationship today between Arabs and Jews—all because Sarah let her emotions guide her decisions.

Emotions are tricky. When responded to correctly, they can help you grow and mature. For example, if you find yourself angry, for whatever reason, and you turn to God for patience and wisdom, you'll grow closer to God, you'll learn about self-control, and you'll probably have averted a crisis. But if you're angry and you decide to act on that anger either in words or action, you'll hurt another person, you'll damage a relationship, and you'll run the risk of retaliation or punishment. If you keep it all to yourself, you'll hurt yourself, emotionally and possibly physically. The outcome all depends on your response to your anger.

There was a woman in the Bible who felt bitter, impatient, and angry. Instead of going to God with her emotions, she decided to act on them. Her choice ultimately affected the entire world.

Hand out copies of **The Story of Sarah and Hagar** (page 102) to all your students. Have three girls read the parts and let the others follow along. Discuss the story using the following questions—

- ➤ Were Sarah's emotions—impatience, frustration, anger—understandable considering the circumstances—she's old, has no son, and has no heir, and God acts like he's ignoring her? Talk about that.
- ➤ Were her emotions justified? Why do you think that?
- ➤ Were her actions justified? Explain.
- ➤ At what points could Sarah have acted differently? How might different choices have changed the outcome?
- ➤ Sarah wasn't happy with God's timing, which she thought was too slow, so she took matters into her own hands. When have you ever done this? Tell about what happened.
- ➤ Why was it so hard for Sarah to keep her emotions in check?
- ➤ Why is it so hard for us?
- ➤ What emotions shouldn't you act on? (For example, Sarah turned Hagar out into the desert because of jealousy.) Give some examples from the Bible. Now give some examples from real life of emotions you shouldn't act on.
- ➤ What emotions should you act on? (For example, Mary praised God because she was joyful about the news of the Messiah.) Give some examples from the Bible. Now give some examples from real life of emotions you should act on.

When you've finished, say something like—

In many ways, women are fortunate to be wired with strong emotions. It means that when they feel joyful, they really feel joyful. It means that when they feel excited, they really feel excited. Of course, when they feel jealous and angry and bitter, they also really feel those emotions.

God promises to walk with us through the most difficult times, through the shadow of the valley of death, through the most intense temptation—which means he'll walk with us through the anger, sorrow, fear, pain, rejection, and loneliness, if we let him.

closing

Takin' It to Heart

Have the girls divide into groups of four. Ask them to each share one emotion that they struggle to control. Then pray for one another, asking God to teach them the art of controlling their emotions rather than letting their emotions control them.

As the girls leave, distribute copies of **On the Home Front** (page 103).

You'll need—
• Copies of **On the Home Front** (page 103), one for each student

quote

"A friend once told me that the best way to understand teenagers was to think of them as constantly on LSD…intense, changeable, internal, often cryptic or uncommunicative and, of course, dealing with a different reality. That's all true for adolescent girls."
—*Mary Pipher in* Reviving Ophelia *(Ballantine, 1994, page 57)*

All handouts are posted at
www.YouthSpecialties.com/store/downloads
password: women
in plain text, Rich Text Format,
MS Word 95/6.0, and PDF formats.
Buyers of *Girls* can use them for *free!*

NAME THAT FEELING

For each circumstance in the first column, write the emotion you might feel as a result in the second column. In the third column write an example of what behavior that emotion might result in.

When...	I feel...	I want to...
my mother complains about my room	*mad*	*tell her off*
my parents complain about my grades		
someone at school gossips about me		
I get a snail-mail letter from a long-distance friend		
my friend says she likes my outfit		
a guy makes a derogatory comment about me		
a guy makes a derogatory comment about my friend		
a teacher compliments my school work		
a teacher gives me an unfair grade		
I'm excluded from a big party or social event		

Emotions

afraid	confused	in love	sad
ambivalent	content	irritated	satisfied
angry	disappointed	jealous	stressed
annoyed	excited	jolly	stunned
anxious	frustrated	joyful	sullen
bitter	greedy	lonely	surprised
calm	happy	peaceful	thankful
cautious	hateful	pleased	thoughtful
cheerful	hurt	resentful	thrilled

Think of three times when your emotions got the best of you and you reacted without thinking about the consequences. Then think of three times when your emotions were strong, but you managed to control them (which isn't the same as hiding them).

Times I lost it

Times I kept my cool

The Story of Sarah and Hagar
adapted from Genesis 16

Characters

SARAH: elderly wife of Abraham—God promised her a son, but no luck yet
HAGAR: Sarah's maidservant—a pawn in the story
ABRAHAM: the guy—who doesn't have any lines
NARRATOR: teller of the tale

NARRATOR: Once upon a time, long ago, there was a woman named Sarah. Sarah was old, her bones were creaky, her hair was blue from all the beauty shop chemicals, and she had wrinkly toes from all that hot sand. Sarah was married to Abraham, who was also old—really, *really* old. Some time back, God had promised Abraham and Sarah a son. But Sarah—who was really old and getting older by the day—hadn't had a baby yet.

SARAH: That's it! I've waited for God to keep his promise long enough. I believed him, which was big mistake number one, and I waited around for him to come through, which was big mistake number two. Have you seen Abraham lately? His knees creak. He has hair growing out of his ears. He can hardly see out of one eye, and his abs—well, let's just say he's not as buff as he used to be. I'm mad at God. I'm mad at Abraham. And I'm mad at myself for sitting and doing nothing for so long.

NARRATOR: So Sarah, being the good wife that she was, took Hagar, her personal maidservant, to Abraham.

SARAH: Look Hagar. I need a big favor here. It's obvious that this whole Jewish nation thing is going nowhere. It's time for a woman to take charge. So, since you're younger than me, I want you to have a baby with my husband. Then I'll take over. Maybe Abraham will have more luck with you.

HAGAR: You want me to have a baby with your husband!?

SARAH: Is there an echo in here?! Yes, I want you to have a baby with my husband. It's the only reasonable thing to do. I'm sick of all this waiting, waiting, waiting. It makes me feel like screaming when I can't have *what* I want *when* I want it.

NARRATOR: Hagar had no choice but to obey, and she became pregnant with Abraham's child.

HAGAR: This is just great. Perfect. Couldn't be better. That Sarah—what a control freak. Just because she wants a baby, I have to sleep with her wrinkly old husband, and now I have to go through nine long months of bloating, nausea, cramping, back pains, headaches, stretch marks, and mood swings. I'll bet I can't even get a decent gallon of ice cream or dill pickles around here. Sarah, wherever you are, I hate you for this. No, I despise you. Don't think I'll just forget about all of this.

NARRATOR: Sarah, being the reasonable and emotionally stable person that she was, got angry about the turn of events and blamed the obviously deserving person—her husband.

SARAH: *You* did this! *You're* the reason Hagar won't lay out my clothes, brush my hair, give me a manicure, paint daisies on my toenails, or run to the store for my favorite snack. Do you know what she does now? She throws up in my tent every morning! Then she lays around moaning like a wounded mammoth. *You* are such a typical male—sleeping with every woman you lay eyes on. Well listen buddy, you have ruined my life for the last time. Mother was right about men—you can't live with 'em and you can't live with 'em!

NARRATOR: And that is the story of Sarah and her emotions.

Read the story of Sarah and Hagar in Genesis 16. Spend some time thinking or journaling about these questions—

When do your emotions control you and when do you control your emotions?

What people or circumstances tend to make you more emotionally reactive?

— PRAYER —

Put Your Hands Together

God, sometimes I feel so out of control. I cry at every little thing. I get angry for no reason. I feel lonely even though my friends are all around me. God, I want to learn to be in control of my emotions. I don't want to hide them or bury them—I just want to manage them. Help me speak and act based on what I know of you, not on what I feel at the moment. I love you, God, and I'm thankful for emotions like joy, peace, happiness, excitement. Amen.

— THOUGHT —

For Your Gray Matter

God wants your emotions to enhance your life, not control your life.

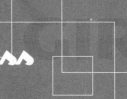

10 | Through the Looking Glass
Life on the other side of today

⊘ THE ISSUE

Young women need a place, a time, and a reason for stepping through the Looking Glass between adolescence and young adulthood.

---

introduction
Delvin' In

Young people today have very few opportunities to mark the passage from adolescence into adulthood. Graduating from high school and obtaining a driver's license are the two most common rites for American teens. In addition to those, *some* teens experience a first job, a first kiss, Confirmation or Bar Mitzvah, the prom. And then there's that first time using drugs or alcohol and that first sexual encounter.

In *Reviving Ophelia*, Mary Pipher notes that one of the most essential needs of adolescent girls is the sense of *belonging to something larger than themselves*. Often that's through school academics, an extra-curricular club, an athletic team, family, and the church. Even if your girls have had a number of significant experiences, they can never have too many. They can never hear, "You are loved, you are God-created, you are blessed with a purpose, you are one step closer to adulthood," too many times.

> Happy are people of integrity, who follow the law of the Lord. Happy are those who obey his decrees and search for him with all their hearts. How can a young person stay pure? By obeying your word and following its rules.
> —from Psalm 119:1-2, 9, NLT

In this chapter you'll find plenty of ideas to choose from as you plan this final session. It's up to you to choose what you think will work for the personalities and interests of your girls, for your facility, for your size group, and for your financial resources.

All of the students who offered ideas and suggestions for this chapter repeated common themes—

> ➤ "We love to party" (as in, we love to celebrate).
> ➤ "We love to party, especially if the party's for us."
> ➤ "We love to party, especially it if means free food."
> ➤ "We don't want parties to be cheesy or stupid or boring or serious."
> ➤ When asked what kind of memento, if any, would be meaningful to them, the most common response was, "Don't get any of those sappy, shallow things that say, like, 'God loves you, now go out and have a blessed day.' And don't get us all the same thing, unless it's really cool and meaningful."
> ➤ What did they want most of all? In the words of one sophomore, "I'd want my leader to say something to me personally, something that was just for me. That would mean a ton because then I'd know she was interested in me and that she'd listened to the things I'd said."

So there you have it.

They want a party. They want food. They want a memento that's thoughtful and meaningful. And they want some individual words of wisdom and encouragement from you.

We suggest you incorporate six options into your closing event—

> ➤ A time for play
> ➤ A time for food
> ➤ A time for peer affirmation

- A time for leader affirmation
- A time for reflection and goal setting
- A time for blessing

Make your celebration as simple or as elaborate as you want. Your teens won't remember whether you had pizza or donuts, whether you played Monopoly or went bowling, whether you watched a movie or rented a climbing wall for the afternoon—at least, they won't remember forever.

They *will* remember the words you speak to them, the encouragement you give them, and the sense of pride they feel when you honor them and acknowledge them as a you're-on-your-way-to-adulthood individual. Your words of blessing and affirmation are the best gift you can give them.

A TIME FOR PLAY

The purpose of a time for play is to say, "Let's have fun just to enjoy being together," "I enjoy hanging out with you," and "God enjoys seeing us laugh and play together."

You'll need—
- Supplies for the activity you choose

Here are some guidelines—

- Play—yes. Intense competition—no.
- Nothing new, embarrassing, or difficult to master.
- Leaders participate, not just observe.

Here are ideas about what to do—

- Game tournaments—spoons, Uno, Twister
- Physical activity—biking, skating, swimming

quote

"As a culture, we could use more wholesome rituals for coming of age...We need more positive ways to acknowledge growth, more ceremonies and graduations. It's good to have toasts, celebrations and markers for teens that tell them: You are growing up and we're proud of you."
—Mary Pipher in Reviving Ophelia (Ballantine, 1994, page 291)

- Entertainment—a short video (bloopers, Wallace and Gromit, home movies, cartoons), stupid human tricks, acting out a melodrama
- Retro Fun—blowing bubbles, coloring in new coloring books with new crayons, gel-pen tattoos, sidewalk chalk art, Play-Doh, Silly Putty, yo-yos, toenail painting (give your gals a chance to reminisce about their "childhoods" through these activities.)

A TIME FOR FOOD

The purpose for eating together is to gather as a family around the table (a worthy tradition that should be observed by more people more often).

You'll need—
- Food and drinks
- Plates, silverware, and glasses
- Tables and chairs
- CDs and CD player
- Decorations (optional)

Here are some guidelines—

- Sit, do not mingle.
- Sit in one group, not in clusters.
- Encourage table talk. (Supply a basketful of conversation-starter questions on strips of paper to pass around if you think your girls will need help.)
- Have a go-for-the-gusto dessert!
- Put on background music.

Here are ideas about how to organize the meal—

- BYOF—bring your own food.
- Have students and leaders pack up or pick up a meal before the meeting.
- Get take-out food.
- Parent-run potluck
- Leader-run potluck
  - Leader-supplied home-cooked meal (strongly discouraged by an overwhelming majority of youth workers)

A TIME FOR PEER AFFIRMATION

The purpose of time for peer affirmation is to give teens an opportunity to practice the fine art of uplifting and encouraging one another—as well as the fine art of receiving a compliment.

You'll need—
- Paper
- Pens

Here are some guidelines to share with the girls—

- ➤ Sincerity, sincerity, sincerity
- ➤ Encouragement, encouragement, encouragement
- ➤ Consider pairing up with someone other than your best friend so you can deepen another relationship. (If you choose the partners, keep this point in mind when making your selections.)

However you handle peer affirmations, be certain you plan the details so everyone is included to the same degree. Being left out or underrepresented in this activity can have an adverse impact that is difficult to overcome. Leaders should be prepared with affirmations for each girl (that aren't being used during Leadership Affirmation) to use if necessary.

Here are some ideas about how to handle peer affirmation—

Affirmation chats—paired up, one-on-one, face-to-face communication. Give the girls several minutes to affirm one another verbally with statements that begin with one or more of these phrases:

- ➤ You are... (*You are very easy to talk to.*)
- ➤ You have... (*You have the ability to know how people are feeling.*)
- ➤ I admire... (*I admire the way you seem comfortable in many different situations.*)

- ➤ I've noticed... (*I've noticed that you act friendly with all the girls, not just your closest friends.*)

Affirmation notes—paired off letter writing. Have students spend some time writing a letter to a partner listing affirmations like those listed above. Give students an opportunity to read their letters when time is up or let them take the letters home to read later.

Affirmation groups—multiple words of encouragement. Divide students into groups of four or five. Instruct them to take just a few minutes to write down an affirmation for each person in the group. When they're done, have the girls read their affirmations out loud to the group so everyone can be a part of the encouragement.

A TIME FOR LEADER AFFIRMATION

The purpose of leader affirmation is to demonstrate to each and every student that you notice her, you know her, you value her, and you're cheering for her.

You'll need—
- The determination to do this well
- Materials for affirmations, such as stationery and envelopes (optional)

Here are some guidelines—

- ➤ Affirmations should be specific. No all-purpose, one-size-fits-all affirmations allowed. ("Your sense of humor helps me look at the bright side of hard situations," not, "You're such a great kid.")
- ➤ Affirmations should be accurate. (Research by calling a parent, relative, or friend if necessary.)
- ➤ Affirmations should be written down so the girls can keep them. (They'll read them many times!)

quote

"Compared with most other societies, ours is short of rituals that meaningfully recognize young people's arrival at maturity."
— *Thomas Hine in* The Rise and Fall of the American Teenager
(Avon, 1999, page 13)

☉ TIP
If your group is large, divide this responsibility among all the leaders, letting each one be in charge of affirming the girls she knows best.

Here are ideas about what to do—

Toasting

Bring up the girls individually and toast them in front of everyone. Depending on the size of your group, toasts can be as short as two or three sentences or as long as two or three minutes. Toasts should be *accurate, specific,* and *relevant to the previous sessions.* You are *affirming,* not complimenting.

In other words, "Jana, tonight I want to toast you because you're such a wonderful piano player," is a no-no. "Jana, I want to toast you because of the way you greet new people who come to youth group. Your smile really makes them feel welcome," is a yes-yes.

Prepare beforehand. Do *notnotnot* make these toasts on the spur of the moment. Have each toast written on an index card that you give to the student when the toast is finished. This says to each teen: *You are so important to me that I thought about you this week and planned what I want to say to you.*

Dear Allison,

We're glad you came tonight. For the past couple of weeks, we've been discussing our God-created identity, inner purity, friendships, and other issues that are part of daily life. The most important and exciting thing we've discussed is the fact that God is interested in every part of our lives and that he has a plan and purpose for each of us. We hope you had fun tonight, and we'd love to see you again next week.

Warmly,

Jamie Dearborn

Letters

Write a personal note of affirmation to each of your students during the week. Seal each letter in an envelope. During the evening, distribute the letters to the girls personally.

If there's any possibility of visitors, have a few extra letters available. Since it may be nearly impossible to pull together a personal letter for visitors, see the sample (below) for appropriate general wording, but make every effort to personalize the letters for yours guest.

A TIME FOR REFLECTION AND GOAL SETTING

The purpose of reflection and goal setting is to look back at the issues and discussions of the previous nine weeks, to think about ways to implement positive changes in attitude and action, and to set reasonable goals for putting faith into practice

You'll need—
- Copies of **Through the Looking Glass** (page 111), one for each girl (optional)
- Stationery and envelopes, one for each girl (optional)
- Pens

Here are some guidelines—

> ➤ Don't sneak in additional topics—the girls have plenty to think about already.
> ➤ No preachy reviews.
> ➤ Develop positive goals (I'll say nice things about others), not negative ones (I'll stop gossiping).

Here are ideas about what to do—

Individual challenge

Have each girl write a letter to herself about areas she wants to be reminded of or encouraged about in six or eight weeks. Funky stationary or border-paper will make this more fun. They should address themselves as a third party.

Dear Aimee,

How are you? How are things going with your sister? I know that sometimes it gets pretty rough sharing a room without feeling like you want to kill each other. But remember what you learned about self-control—when you get angry with her, don't ...ions rule your actions or words.

Have the girls put their letters in self-addressed envelopes that *you will mail* in six to eight weeks. (If you are the kind of person who often forgets to mail your mail, then put another leader in charge of this.) Tell the girls to seal the envelope if they want to keep their letters private and to leave the envelope unsealed if they would like you to read it before mailing.

Individual reflection

Give each girl a copy of **Through the Looking Glass** (page 111) and a pen. Give them some time to think about and write their responses. You can let the girls keep the sheets or you can collect them and use them as a tool for writing encouraging notes, asking relevant questions, and staying connected with the girls.

A TIME FOR BLESSING

The purpose of offering your girls a blessing is to communicate God's love, protection, and purpose for your students' lives, and *your* love and concern for your girls and your emotional connection to them.

You'll need—
- Gifts, one for each girl
- Pastor or other adult (see directions for details, optional)

Here are ideas about what to do—

Gifts

Remember, "no cheese, please," in the word of our teen experts. If you want to give your students a gift as a kind of rite-of-passage memento, here are few ideas:

- ➤ a copy of *The Message* (write a personal note inside the cover)
- ➤ a journal and pen
- ➤ a book of prayers
- ➤ a devotional
- ➤ a collection of short, inspirational readings
- ➤ 6 *write-me* envelopes, good for one letter each (when the student wants some encouragement, advice, or plain old United States Postal Service mail, she gives you an envelope addressed to herself, and you are *absolutely required* to write her a note or letter within 24 hours, 48 if you're sick or an immediate family member dies—only offer this option if you can be faithful to your part)

Pastoral prayer

Invite your senior pastor—or another adult who has a relationship or a special connection with your group—to join you for this session. Ask them to pray a special prayer of dedication, commitment, and blessing upon the girls.

Commitment prayer

As a group, join hands. Pray the following prayer, inviting your students to say, "I do," during the pause after each item.

Dear God,
   As your treasured children, we want to say that we love you. (pause)
   We believe you created each of us with unique talents and abilities. (pause)
   We believe you have a plan and a purpose for each of our lives. (pause)
   We trust you with our future plans and ask you to guide us in our decisions. (pause)
   We thank you for the unique gifts and abilities we have as young women. (pause)
   We ask you to help us be a reflection of you to people around us. (pause)
   We ask you to help us learn how to love you and others more each day. (pause)
   We ask you to help us protect our inner and outer purity. (pause)
   We ask you to watch over our relationships, both with family and friends. (pause)
   We ask you to give us a desire to know you more deeply and more fully. (pause)
   We ask for your blessing as we leave tonight and start a new day tomorrow. (pause)
   Amen.

Group prayer

Involve students in the prayer and blessing time. Let volunteers pray for the group as a whole, as they move toward adulthood, as they live out their faith in their daily lives, as they work on inner purity, and so forth.

quote

"In order to keep their true selves and grow into healthy adults, girls need love from family and friends, meaningful work, respect, challenges...They need to feel that *they are part of something larger than their own lives and that they are emotionally connected to a whole.*"
—Mary Pipher in Reviving Ophelia (Ballantine, 1994, pages 283-284)

Whatever options and activities you choose for this session, let your ultimate goal be that your girls will feel they have taken a step toward adulthood, toward mature faith, and toward the presence of God—a step through the looking glass.

Through the Looking Glass

On this side of the looking glass, make a list of words that describe you today.

On this side of the looking glass, make a list of words that you hope will begin to describe you more and more as you mature in life and faith.

honest friendships

inner purity

self-control

treasured

beloved

HEROES

child of God

GOALS

Resources from Youth Specialties

IDEAS LIBRARY
Ideas Library on CD-ROM 2.0
Administration, Publicity, & Fundraising
Camps, Retreats, Missions, & Service Ideas
Creative Meetings, Bible Lessons, & Worship Ideas
Crowd Breakers & Mixers
Discussion & Lesson Starters
Discussion & Lesson Starters 2
Drama, Skits, & Sketches
Drama, Skits, & Sketches 2
Drama, Skits, & Sketches 3
Games
Games 2
Games 3
Holiday Ideas
Special Events

BIBLE CURRICULA
Creative Bible Lessons from the Old Testament
Creative Bible Lessons in 1 & 2 Corinthians
Creative Bible Lessons in Galatians and Philippians
Creative Bible Lessons in John
Creative Bible Lessons in Romans
Creative Bible Lessons on the Life of Christ
Creative Bible Lessons in Psalms
Downloading the Bible Kit
Wild Truth Bible Lessons
Wild Truth Bible Lessons 2
Wild Truth Bible Lessons—Pictures of God
Wild Truth Bible Lessons—Pictures of God 2

TOPICAL CURRICULA
Creative Junior High Programs from A to Z, Vol. 1 (A-M)
Creative Junior High Programs from A to Z, Vol. 2 (N-Z)
Girls: 10 Gutsy, God-Centered Sessions on Issues
    That Matter to Girls
Guys: 10 Fearless, Faith-Focused Sessions on Issues
    That Matter to Guys
Good Sex
Live the Life! Student Evangelism Training Kit
The Next Level Youth Leader's Kit
Roaring Lambs
So What Am I Gonna Do with My Life?
Student Leadership Training Manual
Student Underground
Talking the Walk
What Would Jesus Do? Youth Leader's Kit
Wild Truth Bible Lessons
Wild Truth Bible Lessons 2
Wild Truth Bible Lessons—Pictures of God
Wild Truth Bible Lessons—Pictures of God 2

DISCUSSION STARTERS
Discussion & Lesson Starters (Ideas Library)
Discussion & Lesson Starters 2 (Ideas Library)
EdgeTV
Every Picture Tells a Story
Get 'Em Talking
Keep 'Em Talking!
High School TalkSheets—Updated!
More High School TalkSheets—Updated!
High School TalkSheets from Psalms and Proverbs—Updated!
Junior High-Middle School TalkSheets—Updated!
More Junior High-Middle School TalkSheets—Updated!
Junior High-Middle School TalkSheets from Psalms
    and Proverbs—Updated!
Real Kids: Short Cuts
Real Kids: The Real Deal—on Friendship, Loneliness,
    Racism, & Suicide
Real Kids: The Real Deal—on Sexual Choices,
    Family Matters, & Loss
Real Kids: The Real Deal—on Stressing Out,
    Addictive Behavior, Great Comebacks, & Violence

Real Kids: Word on the Street
Small Group Qs
Have You Ever...?
Unfinished Sentences
What If...?
Would You Rather...?

DRAMA RESOURCES
Drama, Skits, & Sketches (Ideas Library)
Drama, Skits, & Sketches 2 (Ideas Library)
Drama, Skits, & Sketches 3 (Ideas Library)
Dramatic Pauses
Spontaneous Melodramas
Spontaneous Melodramas 2
Super Sketches for Youth Ministry

GAME RESOURCES
Games (Ideas Library)
Games 2 (Ideas Library)
Games 3 (Ideas Library)
Junior High Game Nights
More Junior High Game Nights
Play It!
Screen Play CD-ROM

ADDITIONAL PROGRAMMING RESOURCES
(also see Discussion Starters)
Camps, Retreats, Missions, & Service Ideas
    (Ideas Library)
Creative Meetings, Bible Lessons, & Worship Ideas
    (Ideas Library)
Crowd Breakers & Mixers (Ideas Library)
Everyday Object Lessons
Great Fundraising Ideas for Youth Groups
More Great Fundraising Ideas for Youth Groups
Great Retreats for Youth Groups
Great Talk Outlines for Youth Ministry
Holiday Ideas (Ideas Library)
Incredible Questionnaires for Youth Ministry
Kickstarters
Memory Makers
Special Events (Ideas Library)
Videos That Teach
Videos That Teach 2
Worship Services for Youth Groups

QUICK QUESTION BOOKS
Have You Ever...?
Small Group Qs
Unfinished Sentences
What If...?
Would You Rather...?

VIDEOS & VIDEO CURRICULA
Dynamic Communicators Workshop
EdgeTV
Live the Life! Student Evangelism Training Kit
Make 'Em Laugh!
Purpose-Driven™ Youth Ministry Training Kit
Real Kids: Short Cuts
Real Kids: The Real Deal—on Friendship, Loneliness,
    Racism, & Suicide
Real Kids: The Real Deal—on Sexual Choices,
    Family Matters, & Loss
Real Kids: The Real Deal—on Stressing Out,
    Addictive Behavior, Great Comebacks, & Violence
Real Kids: Word on the Street
Student Underground
Understanding Your Teenager Video Curriculum
Youth Ministry Outside the Lines

ESPECIALLY FOR JUNIOR HIGH
Creative Junior High Programs from A to Z, Vol. 1 (A-M)
Creative Junior High Programs from A to Z, Vol. 2 (N-Z)
Junior High Game Nights
More Junior High Game Nights
Junior High-Middle School TalkSheets—Updated!
More Junior High-Middle School TalkSheets—Updated!
Junior High-Middle School TalkSheets from Psalms
    and Proverbs—Updated!
Wild Truth Journal for Junior Highers
Wild Truth Bible Lessons
Wild Truth Bible Lessons 2
Wild Truth Journal—Pictures of God
Wild Truth Journal—Pictures of God 2
Wild Truth Bible Lessons—Pictures of God
Wild Truth Bible Lessons—Pictures of God 2

STUDENT RESOURCES
Downloading the Bible: A Rough Guide to the
    New Testament
Downloading the Bible: A Rough Guide to the
    Old Testament
Grow for It! Journal through the Scriptures
So What Am I Gonna Do with My Life?
Spiritual Challenge Journal: The Next Level
Teen Devotional Bible
What (Almost) Nobody Will Tell You about Sex
What Would Jesus Do? Spiritual Challenge Journal

CLIP ART
Youth Group Activities (print)
Clip Art Library Version 2.0 (CD-ROM)

DIGITAL RESOURCES
Clip Art Library Version 2.0 (CD-ROM)
Great Talk Outlines for Youth Ministry
Hot Illustrations CD-ROM
Ideas Library on CD-ROM 2.0
Screen Play
Youth Ministry Management Tools

PROFESSIONAL RESOURCES
Administration, Publicity, & Fundraising (Ideas Library)
Dynamic Communicators Workshop
Great Talk Outlines for Youth Ministry
Help! I'm a Junior High Youth Worker!
Help! I'm a Small-Group Leader!
Help! I'm a Sunday School Teacher!
Help! I'm an Urban Youth Worker!
Help! I'm a Volunteer Youth Worker!
Hot Illustrations for Youth Talks
More Hot Illustrations for Youth Talks
Still More Hot Illustrations for Youth Talks
Hot Illustrations for Youth Talks 4
How to Expand Your Youth Ministry
How to Speak to Youth...and Keep Them Awake at
    the Same Time
Junior High Ministry (Updated & Expanded)
Make 'Em Laugh!
The Ministry of Nurture
Postmodern Youth Ministry
Purpose-Driven™ Youth Ministry
Purpose-Driven™ Youth Ministry Training Kit
So That's Why I Keep Doing This!
Teaching the Bible Creatively
A Youth Ministry Crash Course
Youth Ministry Management Tools
The Youth Worker's Handbook to Family Ministry

ACADEMIC RESOURCES
Four Views of Youth Ministry & the Church
Starting Right
Youth Ministry That Transforms